Change relational and
sexual brokenness

Barbara Bartosh

Book Design by: Jennifer Ledgerwood at LedgerwoodDesign.com
Edited by: Nathan Houlin at natehohulin@gmail.com

Paperback ISBN: 979-8-9858528-2-0

Our ministry seeks to help people expose and conquer the relational and/or brokenness in their lives. We do this through literature, Bible studies, speaking, workshops, and retreats. This achieved by encouraging intimacy, obedience, and reliance on Christ who is our REAL value, identity, and fulfillment is in.

Contagious Overcomers
P.O. Box 5434
Norman, OK 73070

www.contagiousovercomers.com

This book is dedicated to the...

Really...this is dedicated to ALL OF US.

"Come to me, all you who are weary and burdened, and I will give you rest. Take my yoke upon you and learn from me, for I am gentle and humble in heart, and you will find rest for your souls. For my yoke is easy and my burden is light."

Matthew 11:28-30 (NIV)

"They traded the truth about God for a lie. So they worshiped and served the things God created instead of the Creator himself, who is worthy of eternal praise! Amen."

Romans 1:25 (NLT)

"A whole lot of what we call 'struggling' is simply delayed obedience."

Elisabeth Elliot

CONTENTS

FOREWORD

As a dog returns to its vomit, so fools repeat their folly. Proverbs 26:11

The concept illustrated so crudely in Proverbs 26:11 of a dog returning to its vomit makes our stomach turn—and that's exactly the point. This simple statement has a profound message that this book points to, that we all tend to return to the things we have tried to get free from because they temporarily provide pleasure.

There are often reasons that we are enticed to engage in certain broken, sinful behaviors. There are scars that have left gaping wounds that we try to salve by sexual experiences, alcohol, drugs, and other forms of self-medication. If the emotional wounds are not truly healed from the roots up, no matter how much you hack at the thorny weeds, they will continue to spring up again.

I personally had my own sexual brokenness where I returned to my vomit over and over again. Although I lived as transgender for nearly nine years, before that I had several years of sexual sin and submitting myself to the humiliation of one-night stands. The excitement and anticipation always enticed me like a drug I couldn't resist. I craved the affirmation of my ability to pleasure them.

The emptiness, guilt, and rejection I was left holding would often send me spiraling into depression and shame. But a few nights later I would remember how I felt in the arms of a man and would offer myself to even more degradation, hoping that if I was able to give them greater satisfaction then they would not leave me. I should have heeded the caution in Proverbs 16:25: "There is a way that seems right to a man, but its end is the way of death."

It seemed right to me to do whatever they wanted in order to get the love and affection I so desperately hungered for. It seemed right to me that I should give myself away sexually. It seemed right to me that I should disregard God's laws. I thought God's laws were restrictive and meant to keep me from pleasure. I didn't trust that God knew better or that my choices would lead to my own destruction. But they did. I was left empty, broken, and with an even greater sense of self-loathing and an even further diminished self-worth.

I wish that someone had told me the truth Barbara shares in this book, that returning to the vomit will never lead to healing the brokenness. I wish I had understood that only Jesus could heal the brokenness. Isaiah 61 paints a picture of the coming Messiah saying, "The Spirit of the Lord GOD is upon Me, Because the LORD has anointed Me to preach good tidings to the poor, He has sent Me to heal the brokenhearted, to proclaim liberty to the captives and freedom to prisoners." (Isaiah 61:1, NKJV).

Barbara is one of my closest friends and paid me the great honor of being my maid of honor at my wedding. We have been on this healing journey together. We've walked side by side as we process the pain of the sin committed against us and the regret over the catastrophic choices that we made in attempting to heal ourselves. We have laughed, we have cried, and we have exhorted one another to continue trusting in Jesus.

Initially when I left my transgender identity in the trash-bin of my former life, I was convinced I would be miserable the rest of my life. I had no hope of healing from the pain and brokenness. I was trying in my own human strength to "stay free" and to not return to my vomit. What I discovered is the heart of the message of this book. This book will encourage you to not rely on your strength, but to rely solely on Jesus Christ. He is not a dead God who gave you a perfect standard you could never achieve.

Rather, the Bible teaches that we cannot free ourselves from the bondage of sin, but that the power that raised Jesus Christ form the dead can set us free. John 8:32 says, "Then you will know the truth, and the truth will set you free." For years I thought it was knowledge of the truth that people need. But what I missed is the previous verse: "If you hold to my teaching, you are really my disciples."

Knowledge of the truth alone does not bring freedom. Truth is a person. Jesus said, "I am the way, *the truth*, and the life..." (John 14:6). In order to be free, you must *know Christ* by holding to His teaching and by an intimate relationship with Him.

One of the reasons we sometimes see people return to their vomit is because they have not truly been born-again. Many passages in the Bible tell us that we were dead in our sins, and we gratified the desires of our flesh, but Christ has made us alive and His Spirit gives us the power to overcome sin. It is His work in us that brings freedom. (See Romans 6-8, Ephesians 2).

That freedom will not likely happen overnight. The reasons we indulge in our sinful desires is because they are tied to the wounds we suffered and our sinful reactions to those experiences. Often, we responded with bitterness, resentment and unforgiveness. We replaced the truth about ourselves with lies we believed. We made inner vows that we would never be like certain people, or that we would never open our heart again to be hurt. What we intend to be for our protection cuts us off from the healing we so desperately need.

As I began walking with Jesus, He began to peel away the layers of the unforgiveness and the bitterness. Through His Word, He began to extract the lies I had believed that had been deeply lodged in my heart. They had been there for so long they had become familiar and comfortable. As I saw He was faithful to the promises in His Word, I started putting my faith and trust in what His Word said rather than what I had believed through my broken experiences.

As I began to forgive those who had hurt me, as I let go of the resentment, as I embraced His truth and not my own understanding, He was working in me a miraculous healing deep in my soul that has astounded many.

After many years and countless unfulfilling sexual encounters that left me feeling worthless and rejected, I finally surrendered it all to the Lord, committed to do it God's way. For the first time in my life, I began to feel secure in being single and fulfilled by Jesus. When I least expected it, God brought an amazing man into my life, and we were married about a year later.

I was stunned by the vast difference between sexual intimacy God's way inside the boundaries of covenant marriage and sex outside of marriage. There was no comparison; they are exact opposites. While sex outside of marriage was physically gratifying, it emptied me of all of the love, worth, and fulfillment I was searching for. But sexual intimacy inside the covenant of marriage filled my love tank and helped me trust my husband more and feel more secure. It bonded us. Rather than making our relationship shallow, it deepened it, and ultimately because it is a beautiful act of trust in each other and in the Lord, it brought us closer to the Lord as well.

Wherever you are at on this journey, healing from sexual brokenness is paramount to being healthy enough to enjoy the kind of relationship God wants for us. Whether that relationship is lived out in celibacy as a single person or in a sexually intimate marriage, we all desire to have better relationships with others. Sexual sin breeds insecurity, mistrust, guilt, and shame, that keep us from being a good gift to others. But the healing God offers can restore and bring us first into a right relationship with Him and then we will be free to truly love others.

Come with Barbara and walk with her as I have walked with her on her healing journey. Drink deeply of the living water that Christ offers through His Word that will bring the healing and transformation you are seeking. Psalm 107:20 is one of my life verses. It says, "He sent His Word to heal them and deliver them from their destructions." I pray this book is an encouragement to you to return to Jesus over and over again, to seek Him with all your heart, to trust His Word, and to not return to your vomit again.

Laura Perry Smalts
www.transgendertotransformed.com
Find hope and freedom from gender dysphoria in Jesus!

GETTING STARTED

VOMIT, is an 8 week biblical study in relational and sexual brokenness. It's only 2 sections a week giving you time each week to reflect and study more deeply, as needed. Here are some study guide tips to get you started.

- Start and end each day's Bible study with prayer.
- Take your time when answering each question.
- There is a spot at the end of each day for notes, refection and thoughts.
- Join our Facebook community and study LIVE.

Join Our Facebook Community Today!

www.facebook.com/groups/304767760782218

week one

VOMIT

"As a dog returns to its vomit, so fools repeat their folly." Proverbs 26:11 NIV

Classy title, right? It's what the Holy Spirit spoke to my heart when I meditated on the choices I had made before fully re-committing to Christ and finally finding freedom from all sorts of bondage. I heard, "it's like returning to your vomit again and again and again."

This book is for men and women. One gender doesn't have a monopoly on brokenness. So, if you're sitting here thinking, "this isn't for me; I'm not in bondage," but you picked up the book when you read "relational and sexual sin," then you are EXACTLY to whom I am writing. And there will be run-on sentences and sentences that start with "and" because I feel like I'm sitting across from you and talking to you while sipping on an Americano with half-and-half and two sugars. My poor editor.

I could write a comfortable, gentle book that encourages you to live a life pleasing to God because you are a child of the King. And that's not wrong. Since the western church has a propensity toward adopting the brokenness and lifestyle of the world, I thought it fitting to sound the alarm and offer some tough love to help you out of submission to "all the feels" and alluring gimmicks of our sinful world. I don't want to make you feel good. I want to tell you the truth, no matter how frustrating, inconvenient, or painful it is. Submitting to God is not always easy. I don't think it was ever supposed to be.

I'm yelling, "you're on fire!" No, I'm not using the fire analogy to give you visions of fire and brimstone. I see all of us in the fire here on earth, and here's how it can play out:

1. We stand in the fire the entire time, screaming in pain.
2. We jump in and out of the fire. Jumping in, scalded. Jumping out, healing but not quite. Jumping in again, scalded...

In these first two scenarios, you never get out and stay out. The fire continues to burn you.

3. This third option is my plea to you: that you take a stand for yourself. That you recognize the fire that's burning you. That you recognize your culpability for stepping into the flames and staying there. And here's what I'm most excited about: that you make this the last time you allow the flames to lick at you and dissolve your flesh. My passionate desire is for you to now be molded, fulfilled, refined, and loved by Christ—never again to return to the flames that consume your wholeness and joy!

Your consistent, predictable, self-pitying, self-sabotaging bondage is like the dog in Proverbs 26:11, who is "returning to his vomit."

Eew.

But, oh so true! And we'll talk a little later about why in the world they do this, which oddly correlates with why we go back to bondage or ever refuse to leave it.

After exiting another abusive relationship, after a one-night stand (whether it was "good" or not), after complaining in bitterness about your mother over an event five years ago, after the stupor of two hours of porn, after screaming at another car for being in your way, after the fourth time masturbating that day, after binge eating to avoid feeling, after putting your self-worth in the hands of others, after compromising your or another's integrity, after the disappointment of another person not having the answers or being able to fulfill you, after experimenting with your same-sex friend, after deciding you were always really meant to be the opposite sex or no sex at all, coveting, pushing boundaries, after lusting, and after taking advantage of people—whew, I'm tired... After these things, I assure you, you will be right back where you started.

We may have been able to buy some time. Maybe we blew off steam, got some relief, proved ourselves, consoled ourselves, or found a martyr to do so. Perhaps we eased some pain and finally found some companionship. We successfully distracted ourselves, but all these endeavors eventually bring us full circle because it isn't about all those things to begin with. Or if it is, we fill ourselves up with exactly the things we DON'T need, and we start the cycle over again.

We return to the vomit.

We'll lap it up, sometimes gratefully, sometimes shamefully, sometimes ravenously, but always confused. Why aren't we ever fulfilled? Why are we disappointed, angry, confused, ashamed, and even hungrier? Then we'll try licking it all up again. And I get it. We're hoping we'll eat enough of the vomit, and just underneath one of the layers, there will be the treasure, and it will ALL have been worth it.

We aren't stupid. We're broken.

We're broken but NOT hopeless.

And, well, okay, maybe just a little stupid.

But I'm here to tell you the transformational, POWERFUL presence, love, and hand of Jesus Christ truly can make it to where we NEVER return to that vomit again.

We aren't stupid. We're broken.

Believing this will require you to strip yourself of everything you think you know about God. Whatever every well-meaning parent, misguided pastor, bitter or hurtful person, or any other figure that presented a broken Christ to you out of their brokenness must be acknowledged and forgiven. That particular Jesus has to be laid aside. This will free you to begin knowing Him through His filter and lens as you take FULL RESPONSIBILITY to develop a true relationship through the Bible, prayer, engagement, reliance, gratitude, and fellowship. There is a Jesus you have never met, and He looks very different from the fire and brimstone Jesus, the culturally acceptable Jesus, and the inherited or adopted Jesus.

Isaiah 26:9 ESV says, "My soul yearns for you in the night; my spirit within me earnestly seeks you. For when your judgments are in the earth, the inhabitants of the earth learn righteousness." Actively yearning for authentic intimacy with the Father, the Son, and the Holy Spirit will help you learn righteousness, not because you are afraid, but because you now know His judgments are about love, protection, and righteousness.

I invite men and women to be brutally honest with what they have done to themselves and others. This means acknowledging what you are capable of inside the bondage of sexual sin, then forgiving yourself, asking for forgiveness, giving it to Jesus ONCE AND FOR ALL, and allowing Him to make beauty from ashes and reclaim and restore you!

LET'S GOOOOOOOOO!!!!!!!

QUESTIONS

1. What are you returning to?

2. What has this done to you and those around you?

3. Are you ready to forgive and be forgiven ?

ROOM FOR NOTES

week one

DLC (Delicate Little Christian)

This is how I lovingly refer to my bestie. It's my term of endearment for her. She's tender-hearted and naive in the worldly/cultural sense, which has protected her quite a bit. Sometimes she's grateful for this protection. But in other circumstances, she thinks knowing the harder stuff would've helped her out. I am not a DLC, even though I sometimes think it would be nice and less exhausting.

All this to say that even though I do not feel I have to prove myself to you, I want you to know this confidence and passion you are perceiving does not come without experience. Having foolishly hung out in the fire like the proverbial frog in boiling water is why I'm writing to you. Writing this is time well spent if I can get even one of you out of the fire before you do the same.

I will preface my story with an important note: I reject and rebuke the spirit of bitterness, resentment, and judgmentalism. I love my mother, am proud of her as a follower of Christ, and I understand. I am not upset with any person in my life who has hurt me—as a child or an adult. I lay that all at the feet of my Savior. As for some of these people, I am unsure if they were ever approached with the Gospel, and I grieve that uncertainty. But the Lord is Sovereign, and I wholly trust Him.

I grew up in an atheist home. My mother had been burned by an abusive, self-righteous mom, so she said, "no thank you," and embarked on a life of making decisions from brokenness. I grew up objectified and sexualized, and I felt stupid and certain my worth and identity were in my looks and what I could do for men. I was sexually abused by my stepfather for two years. Men, especially older ones, have flirted with me since I can remember. My father was bisexual, and even though that wasn't in my face or known growing up, it became apparent when he died from complications of AIDS when I was ten years old. My mother divorced him when I was five; he was rarely around and truly had no idea how I was most of the time. I don't think he even had the desire to be a father and was simply terrible at it, executing it from his brokenness.

Our brokenness collides with others' brokenness

Even though I never had sex, I did everything else with anyone who gave me attention. I didn't know what I was doing—and I certainly didn't like it—but I was mimicking what I believed I was made for. I kept actual sex "sacred" because it was the only thing I felt I could control. I was SEVERELY depressed in my teenage years and seriously attempted suicide twice as a young adult. If in my young adult years, I had been supplied with a truly healthy, stable, loving, godly person at the time, I am sure I would have sabotaged such a relationship.

Fast forward through a twenty-year marriage filled with some good times, pornography addiction, kids, self-righteousness, an affair, neglect, the abuse of God's word, justification, and extreme brokenness, I found myself divorcing at forty years old.

So, what was the problem? Was it the spouse? Was it me? Was it that God abandoned me? I was convinced a marriage with a Christian was the answer. In time I realized brokenness can still exist in a Christian marriage. I realized no matter what I STILL would have been lost and unfulfilled. I STILL would have been left with a low sense of self-worth because I never ONCE looked to Jesus to be the true Lord of my life, my Deliverer, my EVERYTHING. I didn't submit to Him or take Him seriously. Something tells me if you are in relational and/or sexual bondage, you haven't either.

After my divorce, I left the church. I denied God's existence, rejecting the importance or even the existence of Jesus. I deemed I had gotten it all wrong, and I needed to rectify it by going in the opposite direction. I decided no Christian man was ever going to hurt me again. So, I started relationships with people who could take or leave God, or just see Him on Easter, a couple of Atheists, weasels, disgusting men, hurtful men, manipulative men, one-night stand men, friends with benefits men, and all the men who invested in me just enough to get what they wanted.

It hurts to write that. The stories between those lines hurt so very badly. When I think of what I did, what I allowed others to do to my mind, body, and heart; what I compromised and the denial of Christ that took place—it kills me. And all of it, ALL OF IT, was to distract me from the truth of who I was, what I was capable of, what I was missing, and what I could have. It was Satan's magnum opus of my life.

So now that you know I have a legitimate reason to plead with you, my friends, let's get to work!

QUESTIONS

We live in a culture that idolizes feelings and disregards the truth. It's no wonder we keep lapping up layers thinking just maybe we're off a bit and we'll finally stumble upon the right layer, and it will all be okay. The world is upside down. We think freedom is in the feelings, making the truth when the Kingdom says truth brings freedom.

1. What manufactured feelings or experiences do you tend to recycle?

2. What lies have you believed?

3. How does it make you feel when you read that you are highly valuable and favored by God? Do you believe it?

____

____

____

____

____

____

____

ROOM FOR NOTES

week two

Oh, Why Do They Eat Their Vomit?!?!

I know, I know. I could have picked another analogy, but boy does this encapsulate just how disgusting sexual sin is. Not that you are a disgusting person, but what you are doing to yourself, and others is.

So, there are a couple of reasons dogs eat their vomit, but here's the main one:

They don't take their time. They are so ravenous to get that food into their stomach that they inhale it. It's too much too fast, and so they throw it all up. It sits before them, and even though it may not look the same, it still smells like food. There is a familiarity to it, and since they aren't yet satisfied, they go at it again.

Isn't that like us? We want what we want yesterday, so there is no practical plan when we get it in front of us. We are driven strictly by carnal desire. We don't even check the content. It looks and smells pretty good, so we just GO FOR IT as fast as we can so we can get the feelings we seek as fast as we can. But then, in some way, it hurts us, disappoints us, makes us feel even emptier than before, and so we go for it again because maybe this time it will fill us up. We're recycling manufactured toxic experiences.

An interesting thing about dog vomit is that it's unhealthy for them to eat it again. After going through the dog's system, it has amassed certain toxins that are harmful if the recycled content is consumed. Please be connecting the dots.

SITUATION	LIE		TRUTH
She didn't return my calls after sex with me	I wasn't good in bed	I'm not fit enough	We shouldn't be having sex. She isn't my wife. My worth isn't in my body. I need to look for a godly woman and value in Christ
He broke up with me	I'll always be alone	I am annoying	I am valuable and worth a man loving my strengths and working with my weaknesses
She is controlling	I need to man up	She just has high standards	Her standards don't reflect Christ. She would want me to lead our relationship in Christ
I hate [insert sexual act]	I should respect him	He "needs" it to turn him on	A godly husband would not be ok scaring or compromising me
She flirts with everyone but says she won't touch	I'm just jealous	I'm really lucky to have her	A godly woman will strive to love me in a Christ-like way
He keeps making fun of me	I just need to lay low and shut up	I do act stupid sometimes	Christ didn't demean people and a godly husband trying to love you as Christ loved won't do that
She keeps hurting me the same way	I'll do it back to her and see how she likes it	At least she owns it and says she's sorry	Repentance is striving towards actual change and reciprocating the hurt will just fuel bitterness in us both
She left me	I'm a loser. It just took her a while to figure it out	I wouldn't want to be married to me either	Two godly people would seek God's will and guidance to repair the marriage. Everyone is worth fighting for.

Folks, we can write a book alone on all the lies the enemy tells us about things not working out, so we will return to them again and again and again. The enemy tells you it will undoubtedly be different the next time. I mean, he promises. So, just go for it again because wouldn't you hate to pass it up when that one would be the time it was going to work?

We're recycling manufactured toxic experiences.

My friends, THAT is vomit. I can't hit you and myself on the nose with a newspaper right now, but I'd sure like to. No, no, no! Just kidding... kinda.

A crazy side effect of this cycle of seeking fulfillment or value in everything and anyone besides Christ is making us feel more unworthy and unlovable, which makes us continue to settle! The enemy tells you the next will be better. When it isn't, he then tells you all the things that are wrong with you that made it go wrong. He says, "it's your fault, but maybe you'll get it right next time." So, we beat ourselves up and just know that this cycle is what we're destined for, and at this point, we'll be lucky to just procure a person who doesn't cheat on us or hit us. YOU CAN'T WIN.

This is not what God meant for your life. I mean, He hasn't sat down and told me His plan for you, but you can read the Bible and find many things you were meant for, and none of it looks anything like the above.

Below are just two scriptures out of a plethora that speaks of our intrinsic value and outlines God's plans for us. Please note that none of these plans involve eating vomit.

Jeremiah 29:11-14 NIV says, "For I know the plans I have for you, declares the Lord, plans to give you a future and a hope. Then you will call upon me and come and pray to me, and I will hear you. You will seek me and find me, when you seek me with all your heart. I will be found by you, declares the Lord..." This is a Father that is hoping you will come to Him and seek Him so He can bless you! This isn't just a bit in God's Word for a manufacturer to slap on a rustic board so you can hang it up over your fireplace. The Word is active and living, and it means something!

Last, Psalm 139:14 ESV reads, "I praise you, for I am fearfully and wonderfully made. Wonderful are your works; my soul knows it very well." Does your soul know it well? Are you willing to submit to God at least enough at first so Holy Spirit can work in you and bring your soul to indeed know it well? The first step to this life-changing understanding of God's wonderful works is grasping the unchangeable truth of God's Word. This firm foundation provides structure, meaning, and purpose to our lives. In the next chapter, we'll take a look at why this foundation must be firm rather than fluid.

QUESTIONS

1. What manufactured feelings or experiences do you tend to recycle?

2. Have you ever felt full and satiated? What was that like?

3. What lies have you believed?

4. How does it make you feel when you read that you are highly valuable and favored by God? Do you believe it?

____

____

____

____

____

____

____

ROOM FOR NOTES

week two

The Bible is Not Fluid or Subjective

Sometimes I wish it were. I'm not kidding. In my weak moments, this pops up. At the time of this writing (July 2021), I am single and have purposefully been celibate for one year and seven months. So, I struggle. At this time, I am uninterested in a relationship as I go about the work to which I am called. One day, of course, I feel the Lord will provide someone who is in love with Him, strives to serve, submits to God's commands, shares my values and intellect, will accept my journey to lose weight from trauma, will honor my independence, and will wait to have sex until after marriage. And just so I acknowledge the different seasons in a single person's life, I'm adding the following sentence as of November 2021: I've been celibate for almost two years now. The very first thought I woke to this morning was, "I am SO sick of not getting to have sex. I'm so bored with myself. I am so lonely."

So even inside of fulfillment in Christ, loneliness hits. Sometimes I wish I could sleep with a man. When one of my accountability partners (or God Himself) calls me out, I could retort, "When the Bible said that, it was a different era—legalistic, Puritan-like times. We've progressed as a society..." or, "but I feel lonely, and some companionship is better than none. Besides, I repented." My closest friends wouldn't have any of it. They love God's Word more than me (as they should), and they want me in submission and freedom in Christ more than they want to appease me (as they should). Besides, even if the moment is nice, the fallout sure isn't.

The Bible is old, yes. I'm sorry it wasn't written twelve years ago to make it more relatable or palatable, but just because something is old doesn't take away its validity and, in this case, its power. God is the same yesterday, today, and forever (Hebrews 13:8 NIV); therefore, so is His Word. God and His Word are not fluid, and not meant to be changed by feelings, eras, current events, trends, and whims. Revelation 22:19 tells us not to add to or take away from God's Word, warning us that we miss out on the tree of life if we do so.

How unloving would it be to His people to write a book for only a specific generation, knowing His standards and commands would change over time, then leave nothing for the following generations? God wrote His Word, His character, His longings, His will, and His expectations for us. If God draws us to Himself (John 6:44 ESV), it would be senseless for Him to continue drawing people after [insert year you think we move from antiquated/relevant to modern/irrelevant here] only to say, "Good luck, suckers! I didn't create a follow-up to all that!" God is not a jerk. Romans 15:4 NIV tells us, "For everything that was written in the past was written to teach us, so that through the endurance taught in the Scriptures and the encouragement they provide we might have hope."

Using the way things were then as an excuse for the Bible not to have validity now does not hold up. We look exactly as they did then, except we have more variety in fashion, and we have electronics (this was not meant to be an exhaustive list; hopefully you get the point). So, the woman and man sleeping around with the opposite sex or same sex are doing it in denim, polyester, and spandex instead of wool and animal skins. Lust is still lust. It was confusing people then, and there is no reason to think we've progressed so much that our hearts and minds don't hurt anymore when we compromise ourselves now. So, the woman or man codependent on a toxic person can be codependent with papyrus in their hand just as much as they can an iPad. And people were "triggered" then, just as they still are. What do you want me to say? Years may pass, and our environments may change, but human behavior does not. The enemy can work in antiquated or modern ways. He too, is the same yesterday, today, but then he gets defeated (ah, snap).

Truths don't lose validity because they are old.

The precepts of most ideals you cling to are old or adopted and adapted from an old system. New ageism, Buddhism, and Islam, to name a few— are old, yet people follow them without the argument that they are unrelatable and antiquated. Perhaps this is overlooked with these and others because they are malleable, changing according to the whims of the casual practitioner. Those crystals you put in a jar when a full moon is out so they can cleanse and absorb energy—that practice wasn't invented in 1994. People didn't start meditating in 2003. Salat wasn't introduced in 2011. It wasn't 1981 when Jesus said, "the body is not meant for sexual immorality but for the Lord and the Lord for the body" (1 Corinthians 6:13 NIV). Ecclesiastes 1:9 AMP tells us that "the thing that has been—it is what will be [again], and that which has been done is that which will be done again, and there is nothing new under the sun."

And I know there has got to be a part of you that's thinking, "but what about the writing that was left out? What if those contained themes such as, "as long as you are responsible with others' hearts, God doesn't care whom you have sex with," or "if the feeling of want or love is ten times stronger than that of logic, go with it." I'm going to say a hard "no" to that. God is not powerless and at the mercy of those who compiled and distributed His Word. His Word is active, and He anointed it all, and His hand is in all of it, and what we have of it is exactly what we need. It is not short of any scenarios. 2 Peter 1:3 NIV says, "His divine power has given us everything we need for a godly life through our knowledge of Him who called us by His own glory and goodness."

If you need more than what is in God's Word, more than a relationship with God in submission and love, and more than a Christian community that will encourage you to take a stand, then you have a lot of thinking to do and a big decision to make. I would encourage you to find someone to talk with. Somebody wise, uses judgment, is unwavering, and who cares for you with the heart of Jesus, not the heart of the world to pacify you. And overall, go to the Father and pray for the Holy Spirit, for discernment, for the desire to be obedient, and for you to have ears that hear.

At the time I am writing this I can tell you I am in absolute love with the Word. It has given me peace and comfort, and has taken chaotic, painful issues and provided clarity. One of my favorite verses is, "Your words were found, and I ate them, and your words became to me a joy and the delight of my heart, for I am called by your name, O Lord, God of hosts." Jeremiah 15:15 NIV. I know it is in the Word I find the character of God. I can find the reasons why I should trust Him, forgive others, walk in the identity He gave me, how and why to flee from temptation, and know I am safest with Him. Most importantly, I know it is where I can find truth and not a truth that shifts, but a steadfast, bone-deep knowledge truth!

Take this good word away with you, "The grass withers, the flower fades, but the Word of our God will stand forever." Isaiah 40:8 ESV. The Word of God stands forever because it is truth. It is an unchanging, unrelenting truth. It doesn't change. It can't change because it proceeds from our God who—and as stated before—is the same yesterday, today, and forever; therefore, His Word is unchangeably true in reflection of the Perfect One who spoke it.

QUESTIONS

Treating the Bible as fluid runs parallel with feelings. If we feel we want to do something or need something or someone, but it counters the Word, we have to dismantle then reassemble the Word to justify the want or need. God is Sovereign. It is because He IS truth that we have access to truth and the freedom to choose it. But we have to bend to that Sovereignty and Truth because it is unchanging for our feelings. A world run on feelings is not sustainable and dangerous.

1. What do you currently use to justify sinful and detrimental thoughts and behaviors?

____

____

____

____

____

____

____

2. If God met you and said, "The Bible contains merely my suggestions for you. There is no true right and wrong." What does your life look like, what does the world look like, and what does eternity look like if this were true?

____

____

____

____

____

____

____

3. If the scenario in question two happened, does it change God's role in your life and His creation? If so, how so?

ROOM FOR NOTES

week three

Agreements and Bondage

I understand the emotion and intention behind decisions involving sexual sin. For me, it encompassed a lot of things.

I learned at an early age that I had to run after love. Running after love meant coupling myself with narcissists, users, abusers, and disconnected people. I learned that love hurts. I learned to find my identity in pleasing men with my smile and body (and that my body had to be small, tight, and firm). I learned that sex and attention equate to love. I learned that I was stupid, but at least I was pretty.

These were agreements—also called limiting beliefs—that I adopted at an early age from my experiences. The process goes something like this: experience something as a young child → adopt a faulty view from your child perspective → apply that perspective to your identity → carry it throughout life, basing decisions, feelings, and actions off it. Limiting beliefs aren't from Christ. Christ doesn't limit you when you are in His will. But I do and have operated out of them, and there's a good chance you have and do too.

What do you believe? How do you operate under those beliefs? What things did the enemy tell you were true that you agreed with and now oppress you? How do these agreements affect your decisions and relationships with yourself, others, and God?

What things did the enemy tell you were true that you agreed with and now oppress you?

When your mom was busy all the time, did the enemy capture that eight-year-old in an endless thought cycle of feeling unlovable? When your dad got mad at your irresponsibility, did the enemy capture that thirteen-year-old in a perpetual thought cycle of feeling stupid? When your cousin showed you pornography, did the enemy capture that ten-year-old in an endless cycle of feeling shame? So, that kid who feels unlovable will now base their decisions and actions on the thought they are unlovable. Why would a good, safe, whole person love them? They are unlovable, and they'll be lucky to be treated well at all. That kid who feels stupid will now base their decisions and actions on the thought they are stupid. Why would they apply to that university or try hard on that test? They are stupid, and so they can't do it. That kid that feels shame will now base their decisions and actions on the thoughts of shame. Why would they feel happy and free? They are disgusting. Do you get it? Do you see how unbelievably simple this is? Now those kids are all twenty-five, forty-two, and sixty-year-olds still thinking and operating out of the thoughts of their childhood. And you can bet that these people feel unworthy to be loved by Christ! The idea that we live out what we believe isn't self-help, mystical stuff, guys. This is Satan. And it is that simple, but boy is it complicated to escape.

It's interesting to look at bondage, slavery, and servitude in the Bible. Romans 6:17 says we "were slaves to sin." Bondage and slavery are normally involuntary, or what was once voluntary becomes inescapable. Indentured servitude is voluntary. Indentured servitude was often a negotiated two-party transaction with terms attached. Some servants decided to remain with their master when the term was over. This was especially the case when the servant had been treated well and had formed a relationship with their master. Romans 8:15 ESV states, "For you did not receive the spirit of slavery to fall back into fear, but you have received the spirit of adoption as sons." So, we entered and remained under bondage—willingly or unwillingly. But through Christ, we entered servitude. Submission to the Lordship of Jesus Christ is the mark of God's children. We remain because, in our indentured servitude, we are forgiven, protected, and have a relationship with God. Did you catch the "spirit of slavery to fall back into fear?" Slavery equals fear! But 1 John 4:18 tells us, "there is no fear in love."

There is fear in slavery, but there is no fear in love. Remember, we are loved; we've been adopted!

I find it pertinent to bring up the issue of generational curses. Now, there is a difference between the curses handed down by God and actual agreements with the enemy of who we are. I believe a lot of the bondage we experience originates here. A generational curse is a bondage, or a curse passed down multiple generations or even just one. Alcoholism, Perfectionism, Sexual Addiction, Anger, Stealing, Overeating, Compulsivity, Violence, Lying, Mental Illness, Drug addiction—any brokenness you can name can be passed down from one generation to the next until someone, through the mighty power of Christ, breaks it. Don't mistake inheriting a generational curse as justification to relinquish yourself to the bondage. You may not have asked for it, but you are 100% responsible for seeking healing, restoration, and breaking free.

I often tell my teenagers that our family has so much generational brokenness in almost everything listed above that they would be wise not to test it out. This is the same for us all. Do you want to test what you can get away with to find it was the thing to put you in years of bondage that may never end? The entire chapter of Romans 6 tells us we are enslaved one way or the other. We are enslaved to the enemy who is only motivated by three factors: to steal, kill, and destroy (John 10:10), or we are enslaved to righteousness which brings glory to God and freedom through our servitude to Christ. So, if we are to be enslaved eternally to something, why would we choose slavery to something that seeks our demise? And when we do decide to be slaves to righteousness, those feelings we have, those desires, those predispositions will shift from the unrighteous to the righteous. Perhaps not overnight, but it will happen. I am baffled at times by the shift in my feelings, desires, and trajectory that enslavement to righteousness has instilled in me.

Maybe you will have one drink, and it won't matter, but you will view porn, and it will consume you. Maybe you will view porn and will not develop an attachment, but you attach feelings of fulfillment with food, and you lose control. Maybe you never couple food and fulfillment, but you compare yourself to others and sink comfortably into your righteousness. Maybe you don't struggle with pride, but that time you took pills to get you through the day has now turned into pills being your functional Savior. I could go on and on. You don't know what agreement—unintentionally or intentionally—a generation before you came into with the enemy. 1 Corinthians 16:13 tells us to "be on our guard." For real people, be on your guard! My prayer for you regarding generational curses is that you will ask God to search your heart and your lineage and reveal curses to you and a path to get there.

I often think of Satan as the ultimate plate spinner. When I was little, I saw this on television programs. They would have multiple poles set up, and the entertainer would set up plates on each end and spin them. Once a plate started to slow down, the entertainer would run over and get it spinning again. That's all the person did, run amongst ten or so plates keeping them spinning at all times.

Satan gets our plates spinning, and once he does, he just has to do maintenance or, better yet, allow us to do our own maintenance! It's important none of the plates slow down enough to topple. How easy we make this for him, especially when we do the spinning for him! He spins the plates of pride, self-righteousness, jealousy, malice, lust, theft, lying, abuse – you name it. Sometimes he doesn't even do the running; he just observes as we go. Pick your plates. You know what they are. You have now entered Satan's circus as the puppet, and unless you can topple those plates, you will remain in the bondage of being his entertainment. Until we join Jesus, there will probably always be a couple of plates spinning because it won't be perfect on this side of heaven. But man, wouldn't it be great only to struggle to gain victory over two plates that you are aware of instead of twelve you have no idea about?

I will be vulnerable with you and give you a sample of the plates that were being spun before I submitted to God and accepted the Spirit-filled life. There are probably more than these twelve, but we gotta keep this train moving.

PLATE 1	Worth in appearance and sexuality
PLATE 2	Fear of being stupid and mediocre
PLATE 3	Desperate to be loved
PLATE 4	Shame how I gave myself to men
PLATE 5	Self-pity
PLATE 6	Self-hatred
PLATE 7	Anger I didn't save my marriage
PLATE 8	God isn't real
PLATE 9	Christian men are bad
PLATE 10	No such thing as spiritual warfare
PLATE 11	I am strong enough to fix it all
PLATE 12	Hiding behind weight or thinking I deserve it

John 10:10 may state that Satan is a thief who "comes only to steal, kill, and destroy," but that only states what he has come to do. We can defeat him. 1 John 5:4 NIV says that "everyone born of God overcomes the world." Jesus, Himself encourages us in John 16:33 NIV saying, "I have told you these things, so that in me you may have peace. In this world, you will have trouble. But take heart! I have overcome the world." We do not have to live in bondage, and although Satan can *attempt* to destroy us by enticing, influencing, distracting, and provoking, he CANNOT destroy. Thank you, Jesus!

QUESTIONS

As you read, I've agreed to a lot of things in my own life. I've had plates spinning. I've perpetuated generational curses. I may have created some of my own. Some of this I had an inkling was wrong thinking, but some God has revealed to me over time. Ridding yourself of these agreements and plates takes practice with God. But the first step is realizing what they are.

1. What agreements have you made with the enemy?

   ____

   ____

   ____

   ____

   ____

   ____

   ____

   ____

   a. Were you aware they were agreements or has it been revealed to you only recently?

      ____

      ____

      ____

      ____

      ____

      ____

      ____

      ____

b. What are some steps you can take today, tomorrow, next week, or next month, to remove yourself from these agreements?

2. What are some generational curses you identify in your lineage?

a. List & trace back in your lineage where this may have started. Did it start with you, your parents, grandparents, great grandparents...

b. Once identified ask God to remove these curses. Declare in Jesus' name (citing John 14:14) these curses broken.

3. What are your plates?

   a. List the plates?

b. Where did they come from?

c. Can you start toppling them? What is one step you can do to start?

ROOM FOR NOTES

week three

All the Feels

Somewhere along the line, we started making Christianity about us and not the Father whom our sole purpose is to glorify. We started to say things like, "I don't feel anything when we're singing hymns," or "I can't feel Him when I pray," so we pivoted from focusing on Him. We shifted from singing, praising, reading the Word, and serving to seek a "feelier" or "better" emotional experience to make communing with Him worth it. We have now adopted and adapted a plethora of cultural, religious, and spiritual practices so we can choose from a smorgasbord of self-glorification masquerading as truth.

Are feelings bad? Absolutely not. Feelings are necessary. They help individualize us, protect us, and create meaning. But when good feelings become the all-encompassing pursuit of our lives—our god—then feelings become all-consuming and will take us down. The enemy is counting on you relying heavily upon your feelings. The problem isn't that we have feelings or too many of them, but they are disordered. And the Bible doesn't condemn people for feelings, but it warns us about wanting and pursuing wrong things. If feelings are glorified, they will override the Holy Spirit, reason, and instinct. We often operate off a template of feeling close to God when all seems right in our worlds and feeling disconnected when things seem to be imploding. Perhaps instead, since He is constant, we should reciprocate with knowing He is Sovereign in the valleys and on the peaks.

Intimacy with Christ takes practice. A relationship with the Holy Spirit doesn't necessarily come in an "a-ha moment" filled with dramatics, but many moments where truth is sought and one's own will is submitted. You find this intimacy in those times of prayer, pleads for deliverance, bone-deep belief in His sovereignty and power, scouring the pages of the Bible to learn Him, seeing He has proved Himself repeatedly and faithfully and seeing the fruit of His will in your life. Feelings come attached to this, of course, but they are not the reason for the relationship. They don't make the relationship; they are an effect of it.

Feelings come and go. They change over time, depending on many variants. This means feelings are not sustainable. If we are looking for feelings to be the foundation for a relationship with the Lord, we will be very disappointed very soon! I would encourage you to be a responder rather than a reactor. Responders consider, analyze, weigh, and prioritize. Although they may feel something, they investigate it first. It's hard to do this in the heat of the moment of a feeling, but with practice it is possible. Reactors are quick, knee-jerk-like, emotional, and passionate. This often leads to decisions based on feelings rather than facts. Perhaps there exist moments this reaction is necessary, but more often than not taking a beat first is helpful. James 1:19 says, "Understand this, my dear brothers and sisters: You must all be quick to listen, slow to speak, and slow to anger." Meditate on this.

I mention the feels in reference to God because we do the same thing in our human relationships. This can be a type of brokenness or lead to brokenness because it is not an attainable pursuit. A relationship based solely on feelings is not sustainable when real life kicks in. A relationship based on making us feel good encourages us to compromise where we never should and drives us further away from the ideal plan for a relationship. We don't need to manufacture a relationship with Christ, which means we don't need to manufacture relationships with others.

Feelings don't make a relationship—they are an EFFECT of the relationship

Think about it. You feel that you desperately need to be loved. You find someone who has some traits you're not okay with, but they are willing to be in bed every night and cuddle with you. It's a warm body, they aren't violent, they have a job, and they'll be there every night to cuddle—WINNING! What happens when on day twenty-five, they want to watch porn, but you don't, 1) because you are trying to submit to the Lord and/or 2) as a victim of childhood sexual abuse, it makes you very uneasy. But they are there every night. It feels so good to not come home to an empty house and be spooned in the middle of the night. So, you compromise. You don't feel good about it, but you would rather feel this bit of uneasiness than abject loneliness.

Many things are happening in this scenario:

1. you have not allowed Jesus to be your fulfiller and fill in the gaps,
2. you have settled for less to spare your feelings,
3. you have placed feelings above truth and the Lord,
4. you have compromised your mental health and relationship with God and self,
5. you have stated God is not more powerful than your feelings. This isn't dramatic talk. This is a door that has now been opened, and more compromise will come if we are in pursuit of what makes us feel good.

I am alone. I would rather not be alone. I have knowledge my married friends get to have sex, and some acquaintances are engaging in pre-marital sex. I am aware they all wake up to someone, eat across from someone, vent to someone, and get little random pecks and touches. Once upon a time, I would end up at random men's homes just to avoid feeling alone and to get a semblance of the above. Funny thing is, at the end of that time, I was still alone, and my friends were still married and/or acting married. The only thing that had changed is I compromised myself because of a bad case of the feels and was left in shame, confusion, anger, and more loneliness.

I rely on the Christian community, hobbies, and self-care to help bridge that gap. Bible studies, prayer and worship nights, serving others, having people over for dinner, meeting others for coffee, going on walks and hikes with others, and attending Christian events. I have learned to kayak, cycle, and hike, and taken up exploring, writing poetry, and reading. I have special self-care regimens every Sunday night. All the above can be practices that help fill that gap and encourage you toward Christ the whole time. I don't fill every moment with people and distractions, but I try to create a balanced life of work, aloneness, and friendship that none of it feels lacking.

So, where in your life do you compromise for the feels? Does it pay off? Are you more intimate with your feelings rather than Christ? Are you willing to put your feelings aside and seek the truth? I promise you that if you will run after God ravenous for relationship and truth, you will feel and be more fulfilled than another human being could ever accomplish for you.

QUESTIONS

I know it's hard at the moment to not approach life through the filter of feelings. I know it's a balance of logic and emotion. That's why being a Responder is so important. God can help you with this as He does with me. Like everything, it takes practice.

1. What do you compromise, or have you compromised for the feels?

    a. How did you feel after?

    b. Did it end up "paying off?"

c. Was/Is there a different way?

2. If you took away how God makes you feel:

   a. Is He still worthy? Why?

b. What motivates you to love and follow Jesus, even when the feels aren't there?

ROOM FOR NOTES

week four

What EXACTLY is Sexual Sin?

Sexual sin is its own special type of vomit. 1 Corinthians 6:18 ESV says, "Flee from sexual immorality. Every other sin a person commits is outside the body, but the sexually immoral person sins against his own body."

First, I don't want you to read the above and immediately feel shame. Let's just sit with this for a minute and break it down. Satan is the accuser, not God or other Christians (even though they try [eye roll]). And if other Christians have accused and shamed you instead of lovingly correcting you, I am sincerely sorry.

Do you notice in the scripture above that Paul isn't accusing the sexually immoral person or even talking about their sin impacting others? He is pointing out the harm sexual sin does to the person who commits it.

God's laws are to protect. He is not a dictator.

My aim in this book is not to shove guilt and shame down your throat so you'll start doing everything right and go to heaven. That's not how this works. Following rules isn't going to do you any good. But understanding God's decrees as love, protection, and wisdom instead of viewing them as scary dictatorial demands, will perhaps move you to be a knowledgeable and willing participant in purposely rooting out and rebuking sin in your life.

So, if plain old sin is a thought or behavior that goes against the character of

God, thus separating you from Him, what is sexual sin? I ask this because the answers vary wildly! What I've heard: sex outside marriage unless your spouse is all for it, sex with multiple people in the same season, masturbation outside of the marital bed, masturbation at all, toys used during sex, everything else is okay except penetration, look but don't touch, sex with the same sex, pornography without the spouse, pornography at all, dressing like the opposite sex, unprotected sex, lying to your sexual partner...

1 Corinthians 6:9 starts a list of those who will not inherit the kingdom of God, and within that group of ten, three are kinds of sexual sin, and the other seven are causes of sexual sin. The three sexual sins are:

Fornicators: a married or unmarried person engaging in sexual activity

Adulterers: a married person engaging in sexual activity with someone other than their spouse or an unmarried person engaging in sexual activity with someone else's spouse

Effeminate: the Greek term literally refers to someone who is "soft," but it likely describes a man who is (consensually) passive in same-sex intercourse.

Homosexuality: the Greek term is rare but is a combination of the word for "man" and "bed." It's a man who (euphemistically) goes to bed with other men. Usage of this term elsewhere indicates that it describes the active man in same-sex sexual activity.

Some of you may be thinking that the list above is antiquated, that it lent to the culture at the time but has to have changed since then, changed with the times. Maybe you're scrambling to find the original definition to prove I've got this wrong. It's worth mentioning again—why would our Creator make laws for our protection that are fluid and subject to change depending on the feelings of the culture at the time? It's like He would be setting us up for failure. And better yet, if God made these laws fluid, Jesus would have to come back every few eras to fulfill the law again. God's Word is timeless, flawless, and constant.

Back to the list and Paul's claim that sexual sin is against our own bodies. God is not some crazy, bored, egotistical, legalistic entity glaring down on you and awaiting your next mess-up. He is loving, patient, protective, and steadfast. That fornication, adultery, and homosexuality we work so hard to have the "right" to do, that's the stuff that hurts us. Sexual sin damages people. It damages the person, and I assure you, there will be fallout that ripples to others, as well. God wants us to be with Him and be whole, not separated from Him, fragmented and hurting.

The other six members of this list are idolaters, thieves, the covetous, drunks, abusers, and cheaters. Earlier I stated some of these can be the window to or the cause of sexual sin. We can idolize the body and certain characteristics. We can idolize love. We can covet another's body, or even another's relationship. If we're drunk, we can let our guard down against these things. When we abuse ourselves and other people, we devalue them. When we can cheat, lie, and extort the smaller things, we can do it on a larger scale.

Let's get some excuses out of the way, shall we?

EXCUSES
But I love him/her
I only look at porn if she visits her mom with the kids
When I masturbate I envision my husband
He'll leave me if I don't
I'm uncomfortable in my skin
All the men in my life have hurt me, but women don't
She sent me mixed signals
If he valued me, I wouldn't have to look elsewhere
As long as you're responsible, it's okay

I don't feel anything when I kiss women
Porn in moderation is okay
We believe in God, and we love each other
She is young but acts so mature
Following the rules ended in heartbreak; this time we're breaking all the rules
I treat the women who have sex with me with respect
I always make the guy use protection
Consensual porn in the marriage is okay
The Bible is antiquated
My husband is okay with my porn viewing
God cares about love more than rules
I'm not hurting anyone else
As long as the kids don't know...
A man has to get relief
God doesn't want us lacking or miserable

Not one of these statements should be minimized. They are valid feelings that came from a genuine place—a teaching, an experience, or something read or heard. They may be strong feelings that have guided you to these beliefs.

But here's the thing, feelings aren't God's truth; they are feelings. No matter how real and raw those feelings are, they cannot take the place of what God has commanded for our protection, others' protection, and the ability for the Holy Spirit to dwell in us and for us to be in relationship with Him.

Please don't be thinking, "so we have to be perfect and not ever have fun and deny all our feelings or any hope for love."

No, I'm not saying that at all. Consider my own experience—that God will provide what you need when you submit to His will. Notice I'm not saying when you're perfect - when you submit. And not only will He provide what you need. What you want and believe that you need will change during this submission and transformation, so even though you can never completely escape the feeling of lack, it will diminish considerably and have less power because He will be your fulfiller.

This was really hard for me at first, so it may be for you as well: if you claim to love the Lord and want to submit to Him and have a true relationship with Him, that means accepting His Word even when it is inconvenient, against what you want, or you are feeling something counter to it. These aren't noble concepts being thrown about here. Isaiah 43:7 says our body, our existence is meant for ONE thing—to glorify God. How can we then glorify God when we're running after love, release, attention, pleasure, and fleeting feelings?

I am so committed to remaining inside my commitments to Christ that as much as I love to touch, sex, and intimacy, I am prepared to flee from a boyfriend's house if he and I are weak at the same moment. Not because sex is bad, but because I made a commitment to my Lord and myself, and I cannot compromise it. If I compromise that, it's all up for grabs. I finally know I am worthy of a man, no matter how difficult it is for him, to acknowledge my worth in Christ and in his life to wait for me.

About the above paragraph, a wise friend alerted me that I had neglected to bring up God's grace. That no matter the commitment, the knowledge, and the resolve, we are still existing in a broken world and are not free from enticement.

Please know, that any of the topics brought up in this book, even sexual sin, don't rest on our perfect decisions and behavior. Instead, these things in our lives, our lives themselves, rest on God's perfect love and grace. "Whoever believes in Him is not condemned..." John 3:18. Please know, that if you ever give in to any sin you are allowed to run to the Father who wants your heart, mind, and spirit. He will not turn you away. Don't let shame fuel your practice and obedience. Let it be love and trust of your Father.

When we sin: Stop. Acknowledge. Own. Repent. Onward.

I want you to feel so intimate with the Lord, so confident in the Lord, that your obedience will propel you into a commitment that will completely change your life and the generations after you! Let God prove YOU wrong! I never knew such freedom could come with being wrong.

QUESTIONS

I hope you have gone through this chapter feeling empowered instead of shamed. It's when we are confronted with the truth that we have the power to choose to overcome it! God wants hungry people. Go to Him hungry for righteousness and he will pour into you!

1. Can you list a couple of situations where you disregarded God's call for obedience?

   a. What were the excuses?

b. What was the outcome?

2. Continuing question one: if you had not disregarded God, what would have been the outcome? Think about not only your trajectory and circumstances but your overall relationship with the Lord

3. What will hurt the most in this area if you submit?

ROOM FOR NOTES

Let's Study Together!

We would love to study LIVE with you. Join our community where we create a safe space to be vulnerable, lift one another up, and hold each other accountable.

Find our Facebook Community here:

www.facebook.com/groups/304767760782218

week four

Pornography

I am so passionate about how pornography destroys lives that I won't even attempt to be nice here. Haters of pornography are not frigid, naive, scared, submissive people. I love sex. Seriously, if you offered me one hundred good and healthy experiences to have fun in, I would pick sex inside of marriage every single time. So, calm down. I'm not a prude. I do however have experience with pornography completely decimating people and families.

You will become more comfortable in your anonymity to push the envelope.

It's tempting to wish that soft-core porn is not detrimental, that maybe God wants us just to stay away from the "crazy" stuff that is out there. If we choose to be celibate, we are missing out on the God-anointed sexual part of marriage; if we're dating or engaged, we can at least anticipate it as "around the corner." But if we're very single and holding out until marriage, sex and intimacy is a connection we do not have and cannot foresee having shortly.

People rely on pornography for various reasons, none of which are okay. Pornography in marriage can be a desperate attempt to connect with a spouse, to be desirable, or to understand them. As a celibate person, during occasions of struggling with extreme loneliness, it served as a way to see some sort of connection happening even if I wasn't involved (the Lord has since given me victory over this periodic struggle). So, I was missing out, but I could at least see a connection happen. I'm not proud of this. I could try and make myself feel better and say at least it was maybe once every couple of months, but that's not okay anyway. There is a massive amount of erroneous and sinful thinking with any comfort and validation you find in your reasoning for viewing pornography. And to let you know I'm not self-righteously preaching and/or saying this is easy: today is June 19, 2022. I watched porn just last night. I had to text my friend and tell her. I was so disappointed in myself. I was embarrassed. This struggle can be very real to a lot of people.

Let's look at the TOP TEN reasons porn is detrimental:

1. *You are not seeing a connection.* It isn't real. It's an illusion. Somebody is being paid to draw you in and entertain you to the point you will develop a consistent draw to revisit them. After the cameras stop, the man will not cuddle and talk with the woman. He will get up, walk away, throw his clothes on and go about his day (unless multiple takes are necessary). The woman will clean herself up, and if she had unprotected sex, take the morning-after pill, get dressed, and go about her day.

2. *The people who are entertaining you are in pain.* I don't care what documentaries you have seen where a porn star confidently tells you about their life of luxury and their ability to separate themselves from the act and their life. They are literally letting people use them up, spit them out, and allow others to watch it all. You are delusional if you think these people are super excited when they get up every morning. And if you are a true Christian—not the subjective kind—you will be bothered that the people performing for you are lost and do not know Christ.

3. *The people you are lusting after are your children, all grown up.* These people wore pigtails, rode bikes, went to elementary school, cried when they fell, had chubby baby thighs, and were somebody's baby. They just made poor decisions along the way or didn't have guidance and don't have Christ as their foundation. If you are a parent or care about anybody in your family who is a child, imagine that child growing up and doing the very thing for others entertaining you.

4. *Research consistently shows that pornography is unequivocally addictive AND escalating.* One day boobs or a penis aren't going to do it for you, and you'll have to change it up. You can't de-escalate what you're seeing. You can only move upward. You agree with Satan's lies if you think you are not the kind of person who could ever be interested in orgies, beastiality, gang

rape, necrophilia, and even pedophilia. You will become more and more comfortable in your anonymity to push the envelope. It will also not stay within the confines of a room or on one device. The need will grow, and you will find yourself accessing it at times and on devices that are very, very risky. Like at work or on the couch with a tablet near your kids.

5. *Pornography isolates you.* Pornography isn't something you can share with others. It is meant to keep you in the dark, in hiding, in secret, in isolation. It is one of Satan's strongest weapons. It preys on our need for connection, our desires for sexual fulfillment, our self-worth, and our need for community. When someone at church or work asks what you did this weekend, you can't confidently explain that after dinner with the fam, you holed up in the garage for an hour and a half viewing videos of one woman being wrecked by three men as you masturbated. Think about it. You would never say that. You wouldn't come in from that and excitedly tell your husband or wife what you just saw. Instead, you shove it deep down inside of your head, comforted by the anonymity but ignoring the sense that you are not anonymous to God. I'm not painting a dramatic picture of you in a fetal position crying in shame. Satan is the master at having you "forget" just as soon as you get up and walk away. Only you don't forget. You're being worked on down deep, and it WILL manifest itself at some point in time, usually in a destructive manner.

6. *Viewing people for their bodies and sexual performance will hardwire your brain to objectify and sexualize people.* It takes them from a 3-dimensional being with a past, emotions, connections, and substance to a 1-dimensional caricature. You start to believe that they exist just for you, accessible only when you want them. You are bonkers if you think you will not start treating other people in your life the same.

7. *Pornography breeds discontentment.* You will find parts of your life, particularly relationships, either seem dull or agitate you because they don't look like the fantasy. The porn stars aren't there when kids wake you up in the middle of the night, or your spouse ate too much Mexican food, or you're watching a spouse recover from a third surgery.

8. *Pornography rewires the brain and can impede sexual performance.* Dopamine is released during pornography viewing, much like a drug. Eventually, your brain will begin to crave it. Worse, your brain can begin to reject the

actual real experience and prefer pornography since it is inundated with it. It will believe it needs the pornography, not the actual act, to satiate it.

9. *Your pornography hurts other people* (besides supplying the demand for the performers, of whom some are forced, participants). If you are in an intimate relationship, you are disconnecting yourself from that person. You are betraying them. You are choosing someone over the person to whom you have committed your life and heart. This disconnect breeds and multiplies like a virus. Once, you were engaged with your person, but you now struggle to feel anything.

10. *You cannot be in alignment and obedience to God while viewing pornography.* This is true of any sin, so don't think I'm making porn the ultimate sin. I just know it's a culturally accepted sin that Christians have ignorantly adopted and justified. When we are separate from God inside any sin, we are not in His will and glorifying Him. We allow Satan and his offerings to be our master, not the Lord.

I could probably do twenty-five more of these babies, but maybe I'll write a book instead.

1 Corinthians 10:23 ESV states that "...' all things are lawful for me, but not all things are helpful. 'All things are lawful for me,' but I will not be dominated by anything." You're *allowed* to view porn. You're *allowed* to masturbate to porn, and you're *allowed* to remain anonymous. But being allowed to do something doesn't mean you should. Surely, you've had this convo with a kid before or remember one from your own childhood.

Look at the wording in the verse. He doesn't say, "but not all things are right or holy or spot on." He says, "not all things are helpful." This is what I've been trying to get you to see about God in relation to legalism, fire, and brimstone. It's not about that! Paul uses an interesting word, "helpful." God knows sin destroys us and keeps us separated from Him. He cannot be a part of it! He knows people's choices based on feelings destroy them and the people they love, and that it's not helpful for our spirits, bodies, and minds to engage in sin. In Luke 11:33-36, Jesus tells us our eyes act as lamps reflecting the inside of the body, and what we take in, what we have inside of us, is what is reflected to the world. There is either darkness or light, unhealthy eyes or healthy eyes, and that will show. I had a friend whose husband was a traveling salesman, and she told me he would divert his eyes from graphic billboards. I later joined someone who made fun of it, but I secretly respected the man and wished to have that. Many years and a divorce later, I now realize what a wise and loving man her husband was.

You are worth a relationship with someone who is devoted to you, who enjoys you, who will work with you, take a stand for you, and strive to love you with the love of the Lord. You are worth delaying the gratification of sexual intimacy for the person described above. And that person is worthy of the same things in you. Substance, longevity, and a partnership in the Lord will blast anything a moment of porn can do for you. The connection you build inside this ordained commitment will make porn pale compared to what you two can create in the bedroom. Sex within marriage is better than porn in a different kind of way. Porn gives you a staggering amount of variety and control. Marriage gives you stability and intimacy. We go to porn looking for intimacy, but we discover novelty. If we keep hungering for novelty, we won't even be satisfied by marital intimacy.

The Bible says God will bless our efforts. I believe this, have experienced it, and have seen it many times over. Please choose today to run to the Father and mark this as the moment you decided "no more." Repent, ask your partner for forgiveness, get a hold of a friend who loves God's Word more than they do you, and fight. You can do it through the power of the blood of Jesus!

QUESTIONS

Pornography is an idol, and after reading this chapter you may find in your own life it is an idol, way more of an idol than thought, or has completely consumed you. Seek God brother and sister! Seek community and be vulnerable so you can be an overcomer! Don't let the enemy accuse or dismiss you. Take a stand for yourself and your family!

1. Not taking into account what you know to be the consensus of the Bible or the church, what are your thoughts about pornography?

2. Have you pushed the envelope? What did that look like for you inside your brain and your heart?

3. What are some things that might be lawful for you to do, but you should still avoid? Porn is one example, but can you think of any other things?).

____

____

____

____

____

____

____

____

____

ROOM FOR NOTES

HOW?

Since sexual sin and pornography seem to be Goliaths, people say, "Okay, I agree it's bad, but how do I get past this?" Although not a template, here are a few things that done intentionally and consistently can help you in this warfare:

- Find one or two Kingdom-minded, safe, healthy, and consistent *accountability partners* who love God's Word more than they do you. Let them know your struggles and your triggers. Develop a plan of action based on those triggers and ask them to fight for you in prayer and stand with you during the struggle.

- *Pray, read your Bible, study your Bible, worship, and praise God DAILY.* He will pour into those hungry and seeking him. I think there is a very good reason Psalm 119:15 says, "I meditate on your precepts and consider your ways." Do the same and you will not be disappointed!

- *Divert, Distract, Bounce.* Hobbies, projects, movement, passions, and exploring can divert and distract you when you are triggered. Rely heavily on these. Please note: this isn't avoiding problems. You need to acknowledge these things but have a PRE-DECIDED game plan of how to avoid following through.

  Pastor Craig Groeschel of Life Church mentions often how he has come to practice bouncing his eyes. When he is speaking to or sees a female in person, on tv, or in any media he doesn't remain with that person for long. He bounces his eyes back and forth. I am grateful for his vulnerability, honesty, and the idea of how I can help myself.

- Take a beat, a break, a breath, assess, and bring yourself to the reality of what you are entertaining.

- Claim the small victories. Wars aren't won in a fell swoop. There are victories in the little things which add to the ultimate win. Maybe you sleep with one person instead of three in a month. Maybe you masturbated once that day instead of twice. Maybe you only pulled up porn on Friday night instead of Saturday and Sunday night too. I'm not minimizing the detriment of it, but as we acknowledge these small victories it will empower us to continue pressing on.

week five

Shame

This one is like the motherload of it all. Shame. Just saying the word out loud can evoke shame! I believe shame is one of the enemy's most effective tools.

Let's look at what shame does:

- Isolates us from God
- Isolates us from people
- Toys with our identity
- Traps us in a cycle
- Disassembles our self-worth
- Alters reality
- Breeds MORE shame
- Distorts God's character in our minds and hearts
- Keeps us close to our vomit, unwilling to leave it

If we are doing something that is not in God's will, we will not want to stay connected with him. It's too hard to face. You know when someone makes eye contact with you, and you try to nonchalantly look away before you both connect—but it's not nonchalant at all? That. We hide our faces from our creator because we are going against His nature and what we inherently know. But He is the God who sees and knows! (Genesis 16:13)

If you are not in God's Word, you cannot fight Satan with it.

If we are doing something that is not in God's will and detrimental to our community, we also disconnect from them. Who is going to get home from work and announce, "Honey, I got [insert name here] fired today after spending months sabotaging him." Or, "Hey babe, I'll be in bed in a bit, but there's some porn I came across this morning that I want to watch one more time before bed." Or, "Hey mom, although I'm smiling and spending time with you, I'm reeling over the night I just had with the hottest guy I've ever met." Or, "Kids, I was able to get us this house because I lied about how much money I make." You get the idea. We don't announce our sins. And if it is a sin that needs to be maintained (as sin usually does), we have to stay in isolation to maneuver our world to accommodate that sin.

Shame will remind us constantly of who we are not, and the enemy will feed us lies to get us to adopt who he says we are instead of whom God says we are. Think about it. If that first time you sleep with someone, take a hit or lie at work, you're thinking, "I hope this doesn't mean I'm a horrible person," or "I wish I didn't like this." Then the enemy will give you an opportunity again. You'll oblige and then reinforce the narrative, "Yeah, I am a horrible person; I did it again." Now the enemy can constantly remind you how deep you are into this mess that you can never turn back. And if you are not in God's Word, you cannot fight the enemy with the Word. Satan will EVEN use God's word against you, and if you don't know it, you will succumb. In Matthew 4, Satan tells Jesus on the top of the mountain that if he throws himself down, angels will come to rescue him. Jesus used Scripture, too, and told Satan that the Bible also says, "you shall not test the Lord your God." If Jesus didn't know that and jumped, everything would be completely different! I guess we would probably still be here, but without hope in this world, forever empty, and the enemy's in the afterlife.

Try this when practicing overcoming shame:

When you hear an accusation by the enemy → Compare the accusation with God's Word: see if you can find somewhere in the Bible where God has verified the accusation you are hearing. Spoiler alert: you won't. When you will find there is nothing in the Bible that promotes the accusation → Thank God for revelation → In Jesus' name you reject the accusation and rebuke the accuser → Continue forward in your identity in Christ

Ultimately shame can do one of two things: 1) put us in a hamster wheel of demoralizing thoughts and behavior that we're convinced we can never get away from and that we deserve where we are at, or 2) put us in a delusion that what we are doing is not too bad comparably.

Sure, we can feel justified in those mindsets, but 1 Corinthians 10:13 ESV tells us, "no temptation has overtaken you that is not common to man. God is faithful, and He will not let you be tempted beyond your ability, but with the temptation, He will also provide the way of escape, that you may be able to endure." So, there exists a third option we either ignore or dismiss—to resist temptation because, as we see in this scripture, it is entirely possible to do so.

I love Jesus' encounter with the woman about to be stoned by people just as broken as her and maybe even who joined her in the same brokenness. In John 8, we read that Jesus didn't condemn her. He acknowledged her sin (and implied the others' sin) and told her to "sin no more." He didn't get judgy; he didn't avoid offense or sugarcoat it. He did not placate her as our friends often do for us. The ways our friends justify our behavior out of niceness and good intentions are endless. But Jesus didn't do that. He knew the woman was attaching herself to any man for some sort of livelihood and perhaps to avoid loneliness. So, he wasn't not saying he didn't understand, but he did make it clear what she was doing wasn't right.

Take a stand today. Acknowledge the shame, feel it, own it, grieve it, then let it go and go with God. ¡Vaya con Dios, baby! You are worth too much and have too much to give the world for the cause of Christ to hang out with it anymore!

QUESTIONS

Shame can wear a person down. Sometimes it's easier to let it wash over you rather than fight. But please know you are worth the fight, and it will become a bit easier to break through each time, or even see it coming!

1. What is the main thing in your life which makes you want to hide your face from God?

   a. What does the Word say about hiding from God?

   b. What does the Word say about God's knowledge of you?

2. Do you use the Word, or are you willing to learn to use the Word against the enemy?

   a. What are you willing to implement in your life so you can indeed learn and use it?

b. Can you pray right now and ask God to help guide you in learning the Word, to produce a hunger in you to want it, and to bring people to you to help you learn? Pray this consistently and in expectation of receiving.

ROOM FOR NOTES

week five

Victimville

Let's go on an adventure through a place I like to refer to as "Victimville." Yes, I'm being facetious, but that's because I can't stand victimhood, for good reason: I was a victim for many years. I've been all the types listed below, and sometimes I was too comfortable.

I feel there are three types of victims:

Victorious Victim: a person who has legitimately been physically, emotionally, or spiritually hurt or abused by a person or group of people. They seek Christ for healing, submit to God's will, and build their identity in Him while investing in valid resources like therapy and a healthy, Godly community. They experience ebbs and flows throughout life, relying on God's strength and tapping into the resources they accumulate along the way.

Hamster Victim: a person like the one mentioned above, only they neglect or refuse to seek healing through submission to Christ and valid resources. They surround themselves with other victims on the same path and enable one another. They continuously find or place themselves in situations of victimization, so they remain inside of that victimization. This kind of victimhood (or at least its perpetuation) is often self-induced.

Non-Victim-Victim: a person who is not a victim at all, but treats all experiences personally, and with such grandiosity and drama that they convince themselves they are victims and want others to view them as such.

If we are to be real with ourselves and each other, every human being can admit we've been all three of these types of victims at different times in our lives, especially depending on age. We do tend to lean toward one of the three, though. There are far more of the second and third types of victims than the first type, especially as our culture feeds off of and rewards victimhood. Our society has taken phrases and terms which historically were applied to true victims and culturally hyped them up and overused them; therefore, everyone is triggered, has trauma responses, is OCD, is neurotic, has PTSD, etc.

I want to make it clear that I'm not minimizing that people, including myself, have felt or gone through real trauma and deal with triggers. The problem here isn't the words; the problem is how they are thrown around and used to excuse people's behavior toward themselves and others. The other problem with these terms being flippantly used is it takes away from the people who have a legitimate claim to those things and need to be heard. And, if one's identity is in their trauma, real or imagined, they are wrong. Trauma is an experience inside of your journey to encounter Christ. If we get stuck on the trauma and how it makes us feel and appear, we stop short in our journey and never experience healing, identity, and fulfillment in or by Christ.

Why do we romanticize victimization? Jesus certainly didn't with the woman at the well (John 4), His disciples who gave up everything to follow Him (Matthew 19:27), the women to be executed (John 8), or the man who asked to bury his father before following Him (Luke 9:59). Nor did God with Job in all his sufferings (Job), with Hagar who was set in a desert place (Genesis 21), with the prophet Jeremiah in all his struggles (Jeremiah), or with Joseph sold into slavery (Genesis 37). All of these people had legitimate issues that led them to do or be in situations of brokenness and suffering. God did not allow them to remain victims. He called people out—told them to sin no more, told them to continue their journeys, told them their circumstances weren't greater than Himself, used them inside the brokenness which in the world's view was not to be admired, but they glorified God greatly inside those broken moments.

Let's play pretend. Let's say literally every experience, feeling, and perception you have about your life is spot on. Like, you didn't misinterpret anything, you aren't exaggerating, and it isn't just your side. Everything bad that has happened to you was indeed bad, and you had no power over it, and the people that hurt you did exactly as you experienced. This is my thought:

So what? That's what I say. Again, I'm not minimizing. What I'm saying is I don't care if you are the victim of the century. How does keeping yourself in self-pity, self-sabotage, and self-centeredness—and therefore far from the Lord—do anything for you? If you can't get out of this cycle, I encourage you to seek God, therapy, pastoral care, deliverance, and accountability partners to help break you free. Being right doesn't make what you are doing right.

If your circle doesn't challenge you but only soothes you, you are with the wrong people!

God did not give us a spirit of fear; rather, He gave us a spirit of power, love, and self-control (1 Timothy 1:7)! How can we operate in power, love, and self-control when we agree with Satan that we are victims and should be pitied? I think that although self-pity is a form of self-centeredness, it comes from a spirit of fear—fear you will be forgotten, unnoticed, minimized, and that you aren't valuable. That fear is because you have not found your identity, worth, and confidence in Jesus Christ. Rather, you are relying on attention (like love and approval) to feed your heart and mind. Self-pity is a lie from Satan. Once he spins that plate of self-pity, he and his demons can walk away confident that this system is self-sufficient and only needs to be tended once in a while by running back before the plate stops spinning again. And even then, they may not have to run back because, for bizarre sinful reasons, you've taken over and are spinning the plates for them!

There is a phenomenon where the victim is placed on a pedestal, and instead of encouraging one to rise above it, they are celebrated for remaining there. They are told their power lies in their victimhood rather than their courage and virtue forged through withstanding suffering. Strangely, resilience and power are recognized inside the hamster scenario of getting oneself out of a situation only to put oneself back into a similar one, and so the cycle goes. It's misguided enabling. It's a trap.

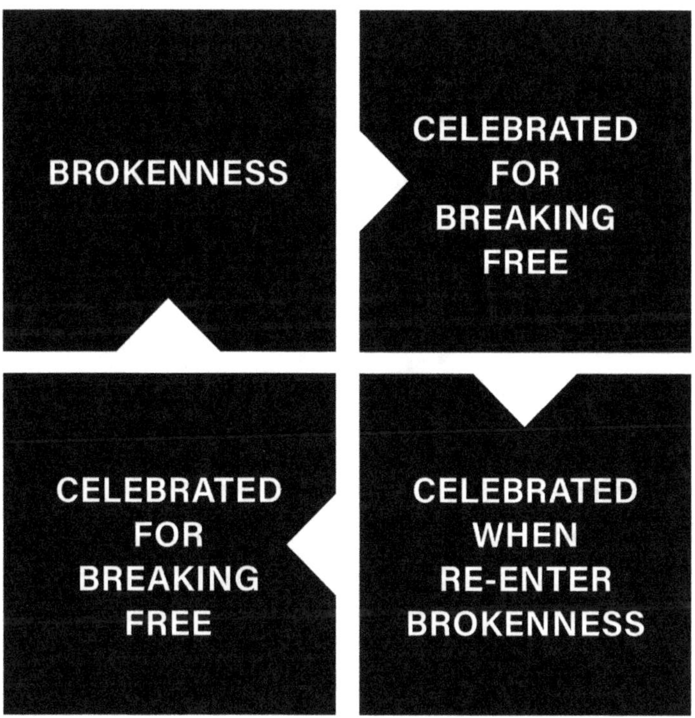

If you are a part of a community of true believers, you will not be allowed to remain in victimhood. It has no place in that community where the emphasis is living life to do God's work, bring others to Christ, and encourage each other, all for the glory of God! Suppose you find you are with people who do not challenge you and call you out but rather only cheer you on or soothe you in your consistent, avoidable struggles and never insist on you taking responsibility. In that case, you are with the wrong people!

Ask yourself, how does living in perpetual victimhood and self-pity serve others? Then again, self-centeredness doesn't care about serving others. So, how does it serve you? Does it clarify things? Does it feel like freedom? Does it open the door to greater opportunities? Does it bring peace? Does it bring you closer to God? Does it further the Kingdom? Does it give glory to God?

The template to becoming a Victorious Victim is pretty simple, though the work may not be. It may take two times, twenty-five times, or a hundred in the same area, but you will overcome if you do these steps and cling to God every step of the way.

- Stop & approach God
- Evaluate & ask for revelation
- Lean in
- Acknowledge & take responsibility
- Repent
- Ask for wisdom and discernment and for God to replace the victimhood you used to fulfill yourself with His Presence.

"For you were not given a spirit of slavery to fall back into fear, but you received the spirit of adoption as sons, by whom we cry out, "Abba Father!" (Roman 8:15 ESV) Don't you want to be free in Christ's love rather than in bondage to fear? Fear that motivates to momentarily satiate and numb feelings?

If victimhood and self-pity only feed you as you go round and round, why not give them up? Why not try something new? Why not make this journey about God and His people and not so much you? I guarantee you will be blessed exponentially by rebuking this agreement with Satan and asking in Jesus' name for God to come alongside you and bring you into a true relationship with Him. You will find His presence, love, and provision will be more than you ever got while being a victim.

QUESTIONS

I am the first to admit giving in to a victim mentality is quite easy. It's either easy to not see it or it's easy to insist it's impossible to not be the victim. My hope is you seek God to remind you consistently who you are. You are not a victim, rather you are a Victor, you are a prince or princess of The King, you have already won because God has already won!

1. Which type of victimization do you or have you most identified with listed at the beginning of this chapter?

____

____

____

____

____

____

____

____

2. In the situations in number 1, is it true victimhood, or does it feel like it when you break it down?

____

____

____

____

____

____

____

____

3. Do you have or can you find some friends who will hear your pain but not let you settle in it?

ROOM FOR NOTES

week six

Codependency

Codependency. It's like the group of kids trying not to look like the one who did it. Everyone wants to be far removed from it. I mean, come on, it's what crazy people do, but I imagine almost every person who has ever lived has gone through codependency—to some extent or another—at some point in their lives.

Codependency encompasses many intensities and scenarios, but essentially, it is the mental, emotional, physical, and/or spiritual reliance on another person. I hope you realize right away why this is problematic on a spiritual and emotional level.

As I said above, we've all gone through it. Think about it. You put all your hope in a parent, sibling, best friend, spouse, girlfriend or boyfriend, pastor, or mentor. Your thoughts were often on them. What they were doing or thinking, how they would react to what you were doing or thinking, how you could please them or get their attention, and what it would be like the next time you guys were around each other. Maybe when you were not around them, you could not gauge or read them, and it made you anxious. Maybe after you did or said something wrong, you were wringing your brain replaying it or strategizing how an apology would look.

Don't be ashamed. It's okay. We're human, and we're broken. And if we are removed from Jesus, we do what hungry, broken people do. Teenagers often find themselves in this situation, but healthy teens move on and mature past it. Sometimes a person will experience it just once, realize the danger, and move on. For others, their identity is so fragmented and uprooted in Christ that they live their lives in codependent interactions. My earnest prayer to our Father is that anyone who reads this book is set on a trajectory to find their identity in

Christ. This is vital in your Christian walk in a cursed world and vital to your inheritance and place in the kingdom of heaven.

We are hardwired to expect to receive perfect love because we were created by the One, the only One who can provide that. He created us for a reciprocal loving, perfect relationship. But alas, we are in a broken world that produces broken people, and we are forced to receive imperfect love while we are here but, please understand I'm not saying you have to accept or settle for broken, abusive people. My point is that people will disappoint you. They will never live up to the perfect love our hearts ache for. Instead, let's not look to people for that fulfillment of perfect love. Let's find Christ-centered people who look to the Father, expect perfect love from Him, and will strive with you to glorify God on earth.

We are hardwired to have the expectation of receiving perfect love because we were created by the One, the only One who can provide that.

I'm not only talking about romantic relationships. I believe the cycle of unknowingly expecting perfect love starts with our parents and is present in all relationships. Our parents were designed to be our first representation of God; their role is to point us to God. But because they are human, they disappoint us, regardless of whether or not they are doing the best job they possibly can, even with Christ in mind. We make agreements about love based on those experiences, and we filter the rest of the relationships in our world through that broken lens. The hope comes in, not originating from perfect situations of love but from three things: 1) using the lens of the Father to filter your dealings with all people and 2) relying on an intimate relationship with the Father where He is the One who fulfills that need 3) surrounding yourself with people doing numbers 1 and 2.

So, your spouse will never complete you. Your success will never allow your self-worth to reach its pinnacle. Your loved one's behavior or status will never hold you up. Your possessions and money will never fully comfort you. Your friends, no matter how good they are to you, will never make you feel whole.

When we start a new relationship with the expectation a person will fill in the gap we are lacking, the person is immediately set up for failure. You have already placed a task and burden on them that is not achievable, and you've started the relationship out disappointed.

People and situations can add value, encourage, help you, and add fulfillment, but none of these things are meant to or even capable of completing you. And that is okay because we have the One who can. One of the absolute most encouraging chapters in the Bible for me personally is John 14. In this passage, Jesus is nearing His end here on earth, and He is trying to prepare His disciples for life without Him. He's comforting them, instructing them, and revealing to them all at once, knowing they think they understand what is to come, but they don't, and that is revealed as He speaks to them. One of the loveliest parts of this passage is Jesus tells them (and us) if they love Him and keep His commandments, the Father will send them a Comforter, a Helper, an Intercessor, an Advocate, Strengthener, a Standby, a Teacher, and a Reminder, all these things encompassing the Holy Spirit.

If you have done these things do not feel ashamed. Feel empowered! Because what this knowledge means for you is you can do something about it. This is really an opportunity my friend! You can change what you know.

If you are from certain denominational backgrounds, maybe you guys have quickly read past passages with Holy Spirit, or it's not taught much, so you don't know who Holy Spirit truly is. That's okay, but the Holy Spirit is essential and worth studying. Recognizing, accepting, looking to, and being in fellowship with the Holy Spirit is what completely changed everything for me. He does bring God's wisdom and will to remembrance for me, but only because I am in the Word seeking His wisdom and memorizing it. Now, when I am alone, unsure, confused, scared, or frustrated, I turn to the Holy Spirit for comfort, wisdom, security, and peace. You can do this too. I won't say every single time I feel something counter to God, the Holy Spirit swoops in, and I only feel it for a second. It can still be a struggle in my human mind, heart, and will. But, at least with that spirit check and reliance, I know I will not stay there.

So, I implore you to get to know Holy Spirit. Your life will never be the same!

QUESTIONS

Maybe this chapter brought up some hurts from when you were pressured to be someone's everything, or maybe it brought up some embarrassment or shame because you've realized you've been that person. The enemy may be the accuser, but Jesus is The Advocate. Rest in whom God says you are and set the standard to choose differently or be different from here on out.

1. In your life, where do you identify codependency on a person or situation rather than dependence on God?

    ____
    ____
    ____
    ____
    ____
    ____
    ____
    ____

    a. Can you see yourself setting a boundary?

    ____
    ____
    ____
    ____
    ____
    ____
    ____
    ____

b. What does that boundary or those boundaries look like?

c. What are the steps to set those boundaries?

2. Think of the origin of someone codependent on you:

a. What is their origin story?

b. What were their resources?

c. What did they know?

ROOM FOR NOTES

week six

Loneliness

Loneliness deserves a chapter because no matter how fulfilled you are in the Lord, this just plain hurts sometimes. Loneliness has no prejudice. It can hit people who are dating, single, and married. It is simply an emotion that hits. Don't ever let anyone make you apologize, feel pathetic, or defend your loneliness. It doesn't mean you aren't faithful or a "real" Christian. I say this because I and others have experienced the pain of being reprimanded in a vulnerable moment of admitting loneliness. Feeling lonely doesn't have to mean you are being a victim. Sure, if you wallow in it long term or repeatedly then you are at risk of becoming a victim to it; but if your response is to feel it, acknowledge it, then move forward you have simply had a moment that doesn't define you. God made us for relationship and community, and when we are without—no matter how strong in the Lord we are—there are days the enemy can leverage it to drive us into despair *if* we allow him to do so.

Personally, in the past, this has been a HUGE battle for me. I am not quite at the very end claiming victory, but I am sooooo close, praise God. Finding fulfillment in God has been a long and methodical journey for me. I have had to be more intentional about this than anything else in my life. Satan has been there for me every step of the way as much as God has. You're probably thinking, "eek, no thank you, then." I assure you, the fulfillment, contentedness, and love I have from Christ is immensely better than compromising parts of myself to be with someone just so I can have an errand buddy, a sex partner, and awesome photos as a couple on social media.

There is no step-by-step program for overcoming this, because a lot of healing is based on our personality, past, and current circumstances, and relationship with God. I will say, it has to be consistent and intentional. There will be days it isn't present at all, days it will smother you like a wet blanket; days it will be fleeting, and days it will seem unsurmountable. The important thing is to stay consistent, believing God will see you through. And claim the small victories. Maybe you normally feel lonely Saturday when you wake and dread the way, but this time you feel pretty excited. Maybe holidays trigger you, but you handled Christmas like a beast! God is with you in the small victories. They'll add up.

Although I don't think loneliness in and of itself is bad, I do believe there are different types of loneliness, and inside of those types are degrees of variants. Also, we all may have been several or all of these at different points in our lives.

Blaming: this person feels lonely even when with someone. They either tell themselves to shut up about still being unfulfilled because it's their fault, or they blame the person who was supposed to make them no longer feel lonely.

Waiting: this person is stuck in one mode: waiting. They function because they have to, but they aren't truly fulfilled. They just know if they are patient, their person will come along, and it will be all better. Everything is on hold, and every agenda involves finding and securing their person.

Unworthy: this person feels so unworthy they will settle for long-term aloneness, or they will compromise what they want and need to settle with just anyone.

User: This person is lonely but unwilling to admit it or incapable of realizing it and neglects any self-work and participation in a relationship. Consequently, they use and abuse people for their gratification. They go moment by moment, seeking a martyr to give themselves momentary gratification with no strings attached.

Where you are right this minute doesn't mean it's where you will always be.

Fulfilled in Christ: this person has done self-work through Christ and has made a relationship with Christ the highest priority in their life. Their service, study, and living for Him make them complete. They are going about the Lord's work, so they are not often caught up in desperate longing. They have their moments, but through healthy outlets, therapy, friends, accountability partners, and God's presence, they get through these difficult moments and are never devastated by them.

Which one are you? Be honest. This doesn't make you a bad or awesome person. It's just where you are right now. And always remember, where you are right this minute is not where you have to be one minute later. God's grace, especially when we seek His will and ask for the Holy Spirit, will supply us with what we need to move forward. James 1:5 lets us know if we need wisdom, we can just ask, and God will give it to us without reproach! It's okay if you aren't there yet, but at least you're asking! Seeking anything outside of Christ will fall short and disappoint you.

When it is a holiday, and everyone is with their people (or you're lonely amongst people) when it is a random Tuesday night, and you are eating your fourteenth dinner in a row alone (or your spouse won't engage) when something happened at work, and there is nobody to tell (or your spouse seems uninterested) when you get a pang of anxiety or fear, and there is nobody to snuggle against—or any other moments when the pain of loneliness feels formidable and overwhelming—just remember, God is with you. You're NOT alone. Indeed, the Lord cannot be gripped in your hands, hugged, or met face-to-face, but He has given us a Comforter (Holy Spirit) who will give us something that supersedes those tangible needs if we believe. Isaiah 41:10 ESV reads, "...fear not, for I am with you; be not dismayed, for I am your God; I will strengthen you, I will help you, I will uphold you with my righteous hand."

In those lonely moments, picture it! On that random Tuesday night, picture talking to God about the day. When you're scared to do that hard thing, God encourages you not to be afraid, reminding you He is with you and that you don't have to go it alone—envision His perfect presence with you. Picture God at the Thanksgiving gathering, sustaining you and reminding you that His timing is perfect. God cares about what is happening in your life! And not only that, but He continues to encourage you, telling you exactly who He is! He is your God, and He fully intends to give you strength when you have none, and He's gonna help you, and He will uphold you! You are that valuable. You are that loved.

Perhaps the exercise of pre-deciding will help you as it did me. When you know you are headed into a day, week, holiday, or some other trigger day, you have the power to pre-decide what that day looks and feels like. You're scheduling.

Depending on the intensity of where you are at in this will depend on the time stamps. I used to have to plan my Saturday and Sunday hour by hour. Then I go to the point it had to be scheduled by A.M. and P.M. Then I just had to have a general idea of what I wanted to do that day. It was a process, and like most things I still revert. So, there are certain times I plan hour by hour again. Here is an example:

FRIDAY (after work)	SATURDAY	SUNDAY (hardest day)
▪ Go to fav restaurant ▪ Go to movie by myself	▪ Wake, coffee, prayer, Bible, worship ▪ Dress, four-mile walk ▪ Shower, lunch, chores ▪ Coffee house to write ▪ Groceries ▪ Cook gourmet, eat outside ▪ Watch something fun ▪ Prep for bed, more time with God	▪ Service ▪ Lunch with grown kids ▪ 1-hour rest ▪ Gym ▪ Work on ministry items ▪ Dinner ▪ Quick walk ▪ Self-care stuff ▪ Prep for work

In Romans 8:38, Paul tells us he is convinced nothing can separate us from God's love. He lists a ton of things that *should* separate us but don't. Don't let your willful disobedience, urgency for self-gratification, depression, or shame isolate you or separate you from God's love. You don't have to be lonely. Come to the Father.

QUESTIONS

Remembering that everyone has moments of loneliness whether they are single, coupled, or married, give yourself grace in those moments. Those moments don't have to define your reality. Feel them and move on. We're okay feeling these things if we don't make them our home.

1. Which type of loneliness are you most familiar with?

    a. What is the narrative inside of those moments?

b. What can be a new narrative?

2. Think community:

   a. What is one step you can take this week toward finding or getting involved in a Kingdom community?

ROOM FOR NOTES

week seven

Forgiveness

Man, this one is hard! Even when we think we have forgiven someone, feelings come out of nowhere to remind us just how much we haven't let it go but instead stuffed it down deep inside or reasoned it away. Sometimes we know we have not forgiven them, and we feel justified - that wonderful, righteous indignation because what that person did was the absolute one thing that cannot be forgiven. Or, maybe you would forgive them if they would at least be sorry. Maybe they have got away with hurting people so much that somebody finally has to take a stand. Then we have the scenario where you would do anything to release yourself and forgive, but no matter what you try, you just can't.

I am new to forgiveness. My unforgiveness didn't come in the form of pettiness, anger, vengeance, or rehashing the "crime." Instead, my unforgiveness came out in cynicism, hard-heartedness, and high expectations, which robbed me of the fullness of God's will in my life. I may not have lashed out at the people that hurt me or talked incessantly about it, but I distrusted and was secretly disgusted. Instead of forgiveness, I reasoned like this: A Christian sins against me = Christians are bad = Christianity is wrong, and all of it is a lie. Therefore, God and Jesus don't exist.

Looking back, I guess it was bizarrely easier for me to embark on a claw-my-way-back-while- still-running-from-God-all-at-the-same-time journey than to forgive. Reasoning, forgiving, and finding a different community would have been more expedient and less painful.

I sincerely am sorry you were abused, defamed, neglected, devalued, ostracized, betrayed, traumatized, or had your innocence stolen. It wasn't right, and it will never be right. But living in the identity of those moments isn't right either.

Matthew 6:14-15 NIV lays it out clearly, "For if you forgive other people when they sin against you, your heavenly Father will also forgive you. But if you do not forgive others their sins, your Father will not forgive your sins."

People don't earn our forgiveness any more than we earn God's

Unforgiveness puts you at risk of your identity being your trauma story and barometer in life instead of being whom God says you are. And when you forget whom He says you are, you can easily operate outside of His will and miss out on His incredible plans for your life. Unforgiveness is destructive by nature, but God did not create us to self-destruct. We are to live life abundantly in Him. Look at Ephesians 3:20-21 NIV: "Now to Him who is able to do immeasurably more than all we ask or imagine, according to His power that is in work within us, to Him be the glory in the church and in Christ Jesus throughout all generations, forever and ever! Amen!"

Some roadblocks to forgiveness:

1. STUFFING & REASONING: What if we felt anger and pain? What if we leaned into it? What if we expressed how the situation made us feel? If we stuff it down or reason it away to avoid conflict or avoid feelings, we are emotionally shutting down or being martyrs. It's not wrong or unhealthy to FEEL you were wronged, to be mad, to feel hurt. It is wrong to wallow, but by all means, acknowledge the hurt and offense so you can move on. You won't die from the hurt.

2. BUT WE'RE RIGHT—SERIOUSLY! This is most people's go-to. And sometimes, we are the ones who are right. But release and forgiveness don't care; they just want out! I've been studying lately that God is always just, but He isn't necessarily fair according to our idea of fairness. In the end, He will dispense perfect justice, though. We are not the Holy Spirit. We don't draw people to the truth, and we don't convict them. People don't earn our forgiveness any more than we earn Christ's. Sure, we can have boundaries and make sure we are not compromised by that person again, but forgiveness isn't about right or wrong, and it isn't necessarily about the other person.

3. WHY CAN'T THEY AT LEAST BE SORRY? I know, I know, this one hurts. For another person to refuse to acknowledge or admit, or even worse, to gaslight you is so maddening and painful.

It's not about you forgiving everyone. If you are breathing, you need forgiveness from people too. If you believe you are only on the end of needing to dispense forgiveness, you have a lot of self-work with the Lord to do. We often function through the filter of wounds, and those we meet interact with us that way, too. One of the most freeing concepts is acknowledging that you are capable of doing some pretty horrific things to people. Maybe you're not going to chop them up with an ax or abuse them, but on this side of heaven, there is access to dark spiritual forces that beckon you. We are capable of deceit, stealing, plotting, isolating, abuse, sabotage, neglect, using, idolizing, dividing, and slander.

It was important that I at least mention unforgiveness about health, but I will not go into great detail. I suggest you research this. A book I appreciate is *Exposing the Spiritual Roots of Disease* by Henry W. Wright. There is mounting evidence that unforgiveness correlates with physical and mental health issues. So, a person originally hurt you, and by not forgiving, you are allowing the wound to continue hurting, taking root, and festering into something unmanageable and detrimental.

Matthew 18:21-35 gives the account of two men in debt. One man owed the King a large amount of money. When he could not pay the debt the King ordered him and his family to be sold as slaves to repay the debt. The servant fell to his knees and begged the King to show mercy. He asked for more time to pay the debt. The King took pity on the servant. He took it a step further and canceled the entire debt! Well, that forgiven servant later ran into his servant who owed him money. The servant fell to his knees and begged the forgiven servant for mercy and more time. The forgiven servant choked the man and threw him into jail until he could repay the debt. People who witnessed this ran to the King and told him what had happened. The King was furious that out of compassion he had canceled a huge debt only for the forgiven servant to refuse compassion on another. The forgiven servant was sent to jail that day to be tortured until the debt was paid.

Why beg for forgiveness knowing just how much we want it and need it and why be grateful He extends forgiveness yet denies it of others? Why do we get to be the forgiven one? What makes us so special that we should be forgiven over others? And, if this is how we want God to dispense justice, what do we do when people are better and more special than us? And if we're okay with him withholding with some, who is to say we will do something unworthy enough that puts us beyond forgiveness? What if a dearly loved one does one of the things you've deemed unforgivable? There is no place for religion, legalism, preferential treatment, and bending of what justice is in the Kingdom.

Do you sincerely want the responsibility of Judger? Have you considered the gravity of the role God has? The weight of it? And because God is justice He can't not do it wholly. Therefore, there are no favorites. Justice is justice and He dispenses it on all. So, if you wish to claim the role of Judge which I believe you are incapable of, then you have to judge everyone, and, with the same standard as the one you have decided isn't worthy of forgiveness. So, go get your loved ones, friends, and all you have contact with, and get ready to dispense justice from your wisdom. I assure you this is not a role you want or can even handle. Why not give the role back to God and rest in His wisdom? You can lay it down. You don't have to claim that role. He has this.

You may wonder why forgiveness is freeing. Because acknowledging this allows you to do something about it. If it is hidden, never accepted, always justified, you'll never be able to do anything with it except feed it and ruin your life and the lives of others. If what was once hidden and isolated in the dark has now been brought into the light, it can be overcome! Jesus said, "I have come into the world as light so that whoever believes in me may not remain in darkness" (John 12:46 ESV). Unforgiveness is obviously not a fruit of the Spirit, so whenever you feel that judgment, resentment, or bitterness, you can automatically bank on it being from Satan or one of his minions, so don't entertain it, even for a minute! And remember, "there is no condemnation for those who are in Christ Jesus" (Rom. 8:1), so acknowledging this is just that. "I see it, I know it, I reject it, I rebuke it, I repent, and I am moving on!"

QUESTIONS

1. Who are you having a hard time forgiving?

   a. Why?

   b. What are the roadblocks?

c. What would it take?

d. How does it feel to be Judger in this situation?

2. Who have you forgiven already?

a. Why did you forgive them?

b. How did you get there?

3. For what do you need forgiveness? **State your case.**

SCRIPTURES

Refer to these scriptures or memorize them to help you in the forgiveness journey.

> And when you stand praying, if you hold anything against anyone, forgive them, so that your Father in heaven may forgive you your sins.
>
> **Mark 11:25**
>
> I, even I, am he who blots out your transgressions, for my own sake, and remembers your sins no more.
>
> **Isaiah 43:25**
>
> For if you forgive other people when they sin against you, your heavenly Father will also forgive you.
>
> **Matthew 6:14**
>
> Their sins and lawless acts I will remember no more.
>
> **Hebrews 10:17**
>
> Whoever would foster love covers over an offense, but whoever repeats the matter separates close friends.
>
> **Proverbs 17:9**
>
> But if you do not forgive others their sins, your Father will not forgive your sins.
>
> **Matthew 6:15**
>
> You, Lord, are forgiving and good, abounding in love to all who call to you.
>
> **Psalm 86:5**
>
> Bear with each other and forgive one another if any of you has a grievance against someone. Forgive as the Lord forgave you.
>
> **Colossians 3:13**
>
> If you, Lord, kept a record of sins, Lord, who could stand?
>
> But with you there is forgiveness, so that we can, with reverence, serve you.
>
> **Psalm 130:3-4**

Be kind and compassionate to one another, forgiving each other, just as in Christ God forgave you.

Ephesians 4:32

Blessed is the one whose transgressions are forgiven, whose sins are covered.

Psalm 32:1

Do not judge, and you will not be judged. Do not condemn, and you will not be condemned. Forgive, and you will be forgiven.

Luke 6:37

If we confess our sins, he is faithful and just and will forgive us our sins and purify us from all unrighteousness.

1 John 1:9

For I will forgive their wickedness and will remember their sins no more.

Hebrews 8:12

Hatred stirs up conflict, but love covers over all wrongs.

Proverbs 10:12

Their sins and lawless acts I will remember no more.

Hebrews 10:17

For he has rescued us from the dominion of darkness and brought us into the kingdom of the Son he loves, in whom we have redemption, the forgiveness of sins.

Colossians 1:13-14

Then Peter came to Jesus and asked, "Lord, how many times shall I forgive my brother or sister who sins against me? Up to seven times?" Jesus answered, "I tell you, not seven times, but seventy-seven times.

Matthew 18:21-22

In him we have redemption through his blood, the forgiveness of sins, in accordance with the riches of God's grace that he lavished on us. With all wisdom and understanding...

Ephesians 1:7-8

ROOM FOR NOTES

week eight

Trust

I saw a meme the other day that read, "Therapist: 'you need to let people in.' Me: 'It's not locked,'" above the picture of a door, and covering the doorknob was a cactus. I feel we even do this with the Father. "Sure, I trust you. Sure, we have a relationship." And even though He knows our hearts and thoughts, we still somehow think we can let Him through the doorway just a bit but no further. That way, we are letting Him in, but we maintain control—or at least the illusion of control. And if we do this with the Father, we will do it with others.

Our hearts, spirit, and mind are hardwired to desire and bask in the perfect love. Yet here we are, in a broken world, receiving scraps of a broken love, feeling lucky. So not only are we unfilled, but we can't trust a love that is wounded and imperfect. But we try. Not knowing of or forgetting Christ, we look for someone whom we can trust to provide perfect love, and we are disappointed when even a good person doing their best can't be completely trusted because of their imperfection.

Most distrust originates from our parents or the people charged with our care. They are the first to introduce us to imperfect love. They fail us out of their learning curve and wounds. Nonetheless, it starts us on the journey away from God's perfect love in a world of the imperfect, so we start moving away from our hardwiring and accepting the substitute. We slowly learn and re-wire what we should expect of people and what we should not. We learn to wait for the other shoe to drop. We wait for disappointment. So, we get confused about what is appropriate, what should be expected, and what we deserve.

As we get further away from God's perfect love and maneuver in the imperfect, we tend to view and filter our Father through the lens of the people who have hurt us. Whether you were aware or not, your view of God began to shift. Where God was once the security, the sense, the comfort, and the covering, He is now a dictator, or absent, or angry, or disappointed, or wanting you to fail. It isn't until we are immersed in His Word—which will tell us the truth—and embrace a genuinely intimate relationship with Him that we will re-learn that it is His perfect love we can turn our heads toward; and that, although we can't always trust the broken people around us, we can trust Him. Most importantly, we will come to understand that even the best people who faithfully reflect Christ should not be substitutes for Him, and they still, in their goodness, cannot live out His perfect love. We can trust people if Christ is our hope, and His character and truth are our points of reference.

We can trust people if Christ is our hope and our barometer.

Please know the above is not saying, "all people are awful, and nobody can be trusted." In Christ, we know our worth. We know there is a truth to us and a purpose for us. Therefore, we will filter people and situations through this. We know we are loved, protected, and comforted. We know we can trust God because He says so, and He has proven Himself over and over again. He hasn't proven Himself by giving us what we want. He has proven Himself by being God. So, if we know all these things about ourselves, we can trust that if we give our hearts to someone—not in ignorance and flippancy—but give our hearts to a healthy person in a healthy way for healthy reasons, we can trust that no matter what, God is going to care for us. Notice I didn't say, He will make it all better all the time. Instead, He will not let you fall if you are in Him, seeking Him, loving Him first and foremost. We can be encouraged by Psalm 121:3, paraphrased: God will take care of us, He will not let us fall, He will keep us safe, and He will not sleep to do so!

I don't trust people. My worldly self says, "don't tell them what you need because they will not only not fulfill it, but you are wrong for wanting it. They will tell you all the reasons you shouldn't want it or need it, so why stir that all up? You're fine." I do this with women and men, young and old. I learned these things from the following people: my father rarely visited and was flippant at best. Wants or needs involving him were moot. My mother was disconnected, dealing with her stuff. So, she made sure our material needs were met: a roof over our heads, clothes, and food. My stepfather confused me because he took care of my needs and wants while keeping me as a girlfriend. Then my marriage reinforced all the things I learned in childhood.

This is what I say about the pivotal people in life that initially caused me to distrust—I'm still responsible for learning to trust again. I am now aware that everyone is doing the best they can with the knowledge and resources they have at the time. Although this understanding doesn't excuse sinful behavior, it brings clarity. And I know that I need God's grace just as much as they do. Maybe not for the same things, but I need it, too, nonetheless. I will not allow the enemy to win by isolating me in my fears. I just absolutely will not do it. So, I trust until someone gives me a reason not to. And I have two very close Godly friends that are walking this road with me and understand my struggle and try to work with me within those confines as I do the same for them and their struggles. They are much quicker to give me grace than I give, but I'm learning!

We don't just need to learn to trust people, more importantly, we need to trust God. It is in trusting Him that our hearts soften and learn to trust others. Just because we have examples of why not to trust people, doesn't mean we should not exercise that muscle and practice so we may find the true freedom it brings. Maybe you are afraid to trust God because you feel He put you into situations or didn't help you. You are in a broken world and God can love you where you are, but he cannot take you out of experiencing the broken world while you are in it. One of the most incredible things about trusting God is knowing whether you are in a valley, on a mountain, in lack, or abundance, suffering loss, experiencing joy, having clarity, or feeling confused, can trust His consistent character. If you stay in His will, He will see you through. It may not look as you believe it should and the outcome may be quite unexpected, but it is always good because He loves you and because he is Sovereign and Just.

It is in trusting Him that our hearts soften and learn to trust others.

One of the more popular scriptures on trust is Proverbs 3:5-6 NIV. "Trust in the Lord with all your heart and lean not on your own understanding; in all your ways submit to him, and he will make your paths straight." Do me a favor – take a week and break this verse down. Find the places in the Bible that relate to and back this scripture. You will find yourself going down a rabbit hole of learning your role vs God's role, your understanding vs God's understanding, submission from fear and ignorance vs submission from reverence and awe, what a straight path is vs a crooked path, and just what trusting God means.

Very recently God asked me to give Him my dreams. There are a lot of implications for that request. I was stunned, I grieved, and I threw a couple of tantrums because what He is asking of me is huge. Because I have made it a habit of trusting him with the smaller things, He is now calling me to trust Him with the big things. Because He has proved Himself before I have no reason to believe He will not continue. I now understand what He requested is not a life sentence, rather it is a reward and an assignment that I am humbled, excited, and joyful to receive. I trust Him, I do. I want you to as well because it feels amazing.

I know sometimes we read scriptures that proclaim trust in God, and we think it sounds nice but seems a bit cliche, like it's something we're supposed to say, but don't necessarily stand on that truth. Like a lot of things, trust is a simple concept, not so simple a practice. But that's what it takes—practice. Practice trusting. I wholeheartedly believe that as you practice and experience trust in the Father, it will become more instinctual as time goes on, and that will spill over into your worldly relationships. Let Him be your archetype (an original model or type after which other similar things are patterned; a prototype). Isaiah 43:2 ESV says, "When you pass through the waters, I will be with you; and through the rivers, they shall not overwhelm you; when you walk through fire, you shall not be burned, and the flame shall not consume you." TRUST HIM!

QUESTIONS

Trusting God helps you trust people. Can you practice giving God one small thing this week to trust in Him? Daily and frequently practice giving it over to Him in prayer, in proclaiming it with scripture, in letting go, and even being excited about what He will do with it!

1. Do you truly trust God in your life?

    a. What does that look like in your daily walk, in your heart and mind?

b. How can you build upon that? Is there something bigger to give Him?

2. Do you not trust God at all?

a. What does that look like in your daily walk, in your heart and mind?

b. Can you start with just one small thing?

____

____

____

____

____

____

____

3. How can you filter the people you allow in your life to be trustworthy?

____

____

____

____

____

____

____

ACTION STEP

> Trust in the Lord with all your heart and lean not on your own understanding; in all your ways submit to him, and he will make your paths straight.
>
> **Proverbs 3:5-6 NIV**

Take a week and break this verse down. Find the places in the Bible that relate to and back this scripture. You will find yourself going down a rabbit hole of learning your role vs God's role, your understanding vs God's understanding, submission from fear and ignorance vs submission from reverence and awe, what a straight path is vs a crooked path, and just what trusting God means.

ROOM FOR NOTES

week eight

Deliverance

Don't worry; I'm not gonna try and convince you to handle snakes (heh. Please don't be mad at me, snake handlers). Deliverance has a bad rap, but it shouldn't. If you can go so far as to believe in God and believe in salvation from sin, then the concept of deliverance can't be that far-fetched to you—just throw away your preconceptions.

To deliver is to bring or surrender an object or person to a proper place. I believe many people who have accepted Jesus Christ leave it at that because they think, "Hey, I'm washed of my sins— yay!" And maybe you can't lose that salvation (we're not gonna defend that now), but following Christ is a lifelong commitment. In Matthew 16:24 ESV, Jesus doesn't say, "Thanks for the follow!" and move on. He says quite the opposite: "...if anyone would come after me, let him deny himself and take up his cross and follow me."

In Luke 10:19 ESV, Jesus says, "Behold, I have given you authority to tread on serpents and scorpions, and over all the power of the enemy, and nothing shall hurt you." This is the opposite of passive, the opposite of our normal mindset. Whether we'd admit it or not, we often wake up wondering what the enemy has in store for us. Like, we're waiting to see what and how we need to defend ourselves for the day instead of taking the day under the authority of Christ and the authority given to us and stating, "you're doing nothing today, Satan."

My cross, my burden was several things: codependency, loneliness, and injustice which led to a distorted identity, searching for love in everyone, and feeling like a victim. I said "yes" to Jesus without any understanding that I was being presented with an opportunity to have an intimate relationship marked by perfect love. Instead, I put Him on a shelf and went about my regularly scheduled programming, just grateful I wouldn't see hell. Funny thing, I was living in a hell I created here on earth, as a "saved" person no less!

If I had known better or had guidance after accepting Jesus, I would have followed with, "My cross is I feel such lack in my heart and such low self-worth and such trauma and such fear that I'm making horrible choices. But I'm picking it up, Father, and I will deny myself all those acceptances and agreements I've made with the enemy regarding them, and I will submit to Your will and seek the purpose You have for my life and learn to let You love me with perfect love."

So, I would've continued to struggle, but under the authority and shield of Christ Jesus, the comfort and discernment of the Holy Spirit, and the love of my Creator. Spiritual warfare isn't easy, but it does have ultimate victory and is better than floundering for the enemy's entertainment. I have been practicing submission and denial of self for the last three years as of this writing. The Father has given me victory over the above crosses. They creep up occasionally, but practicing deliverance, which I will explain later, ensures I will never be dominated. Because this is spiritual warfare, the enemy does pivot when you claim victory. I wish I could tell you that if you eradicate your burdens, you are free forever. But the enemy has come to "steal and kill and destroy" (John 10:10), so he will methodically work and find other things to win you over. As we've learned throughout this study, if you are centered on your pain, your wants, and your cycle—you don't glorify God, you don't bring others to Him, and you don't live out God's purpose for your life. Remember, you are going to only do one of two things: live out Satan's purpose for your life or live out God's purpose for your life. There is quite literally no other option.

I'll share with you what has given me freedom, empowerment, and intimacy with the Father. REJECT, REBUKE, REPENT, RENOUNCE. I just want to be vulnerable and share with you one of the biggest crosses I took up in following Jesus. Toward the end of my marriage, I had an extramarital affair. When it broke up I was devastated. I believe I loved him, and he was all I needed. I had to live life though so in pain I functioned, and the pain and thoughts of him and the loss did wane some, but I was never fully released. Even after two years and a couple of relationships, I was still in a lot of pain.

Just the other week, I thought of a sexual encounter with him, and just the other day, I thought of the residual love that creeps up for him. The enemy would have loved it if I gave into those scenes and lusted after him more, tried to contact him, or entertained whatever else got dredged up. The enemy would have loved it if I felt immense shame and decided I don't deserve love. But instead, I rested in the knowledge and trust I have in the Lord. Through the power of Christ, my desire to die to self, and for my betterment, I said "NO!" After many times of this, I am thrilled to announce this isn't even on my radar anymore!

REJECT . REBUKE . REPENT . RENOUNCE

When I am practicing deliverance, I say out loud, "In the name and authority of Christ Jesus, I REJECT and REBUKE all images and feelings that come with [insert name here]. I REPENT of this, and I RENOUNCE this thinking as a dead work." Do I repent because I feel shame and I'm afraid God will strike me down? No! "Repent" in the original Greek simply means to "change one's mind, attitude, and purpose." People hear "repent," and they're thinking of the fire and brimstone preachers yelling and hammering the pulpit. I repent because I am changing the way I feel about this situation. I am sorry I feel this way because it's hurtful on so many levels. Just in case you don't know, "renounce" means to "give up, declare, decide." If good works exist inside of submission to Christ, then bad works exist inside of submission to Satan. So, I renounce my sins as dead works. It is a work, a "bad" work that has no place in the kingdom of God, so I'm done with it!

There are times I have to do these four things multiple times a day about various things. Sometimes I go a week doing this on one stupid thing! And what I have found is a burden lifted and freedom I will never be able to describe to you. You truly have to experience it to know it, and God does not alienate anyone, so this power is available for all. It takes nothing special except conviction, commitment, and belief.

Something I have found *essential* in overcoming bondage through the practice of deliverance is **Scripture memorization**. Study the Word, and not surface-level, feel-good devotionals. Pick Scripture apart, pray for wisdom and discernment, and apply it to your life. The thing is, Jesus himself tells us in John 14:26 that we are given a "comforter, the Holy Spirit, Whom the Father will send in My name, He will teach you all things. And He will bring to your remembrance everything I have told you." This right here is incredibly encouraging to me! Jesus left to be with the Father and to prepare a place for us, but we were left with an advocate, a partner, and a teacher Who will help us during His absence. This is critical, so please re-read: we cannot be instructed, have discernment, or have the knowledge, and the Word of God brought to our remembrance if we don't know the Word of God and what it says. You can't fight for yourself alongside the Holy Spirit if you lack relationship and knowledge. For example, how will you know what to say when presented with an opportunity to gossip without the help of the Holy Spirit? But through the wisdom of the Counselor whom Jesus has sent, we can say something like this: "Jesus, you said if I ask for anything in your name, you will give it to me, and I believe that, so in the name and authority of Jesus Christ I reject and rebuke the spirit of gossip and I renounce it as a dead work in my life. I repent of this way. Your Word tells me that 'even so the tongue is a little member, and it can boast of great things. See how much wood or how great a forest a tiny spark can set ablaze' (James 3:5 AMPC). Thank you, Father. Amen!"

Try it. Give it a shot, and do it consistently, and Satan and bondage will look very different to you, and the authority and confidence you have in Christ will only build each time this is practiced. You don't have to be a scholar. There are all kinds of resources and apps available. It may take you five months; it may even take you two years to get this down, but it will bless you and those around you. You don't have to memorize a thousand verses; just memorize verses that speak to your struggle. Maybe you start off memorizing a verse, not five or a chapter. I was a bit ambitious in my need and desire to escape entering into relationships to justify sex, so I learned 1 Corinthians 6:12-20. It's a long one, but it encapsulated a whole lot of what I struggled with. And in times of struggle, the Holy Spirit indeed brought to remembrance that scripture, and it was a comfort.

You really can be delivered, even from the disgusting, gut-wrenching, soul-sucking stuff that keeps you bound. "Little children, you are from God and have overcome them, for he who is in you is greater than he who is in the world." 1 John 4:4 ESV.

QUESTIONS

Deliverance sometimes has a bad rap or people fear it. But, it's right to believe in deliverance. God is limitless, and He gave us Holy Spirit and the authority to be limitless for His purposes too.

1. What's your burden? Your cross?

2. What's your take on deliverance?

3. What in your life are you willing daily to reject, rebuke, repent, and renounce until it is merely a memory of your former self?

4. Will you commit yourself to Bible memorization?

ROOM FOR NOTES

I Guess We're Done

Keep in mind that everything presented in this Bible study can be put into this perspective: this world, your little world, your feelings, your experiences, your desires—in the end...

IT'S NOT ABOUT YOU...

"everyone who is called by my name,
everyone I created for my glory,
everyone I formed,
yes, everyone, I have made."

Isaiah 43:7 EHV

You were made for God's glory. You weren't made to be comfortable or beautiful, to have an abundance of successes, feel great, or win at life. Sure, you may experience those things along with some heartbreak and pain, but you weren't made for all that. You were made for God's glory. So, leave the vomit, take up your cross, and follow Jesus. Bask in the light and freedom of following Him. It sure beats crawling back for those disgusting seconds.

GOD BLESS YOU MY FRIENDS
—Barb

Author Page

ABOUT THE MINISTRY & AUTHOR

Contagious Overcomers Ministry was founded by author, teacher, and speaker Barbara Bartosh. It's led by a Bible believing, Jesus serving board of directors. Our ministry seeks to come alongside people ready to shed the identity of bondage and brokenness and claim their identity, value, and purpose in Christ.

The Founder fought to overcome her own relational and sexual bondage. She realized looking for identity, value, and purpose in other people and experiences was an empty, disappointing, and oftentimes painful pursuit. It is from the heart of revelation, obedience, surrender, and intimacy with Christ that Contagious Overcomers was formed. Perhaps people can entirely bypass, or at least lessen, their participation in this fruitless cycle of pain, confusion, and fear. God as Sovereign in our lives is the only way to live.

Contagious Overcomers produces books and studies that are rough, raw, and embedded in Truth so that readers expose, acknowledge, and reject their traps of brokenness. The ministry also offers discipleship, speaking, workshops, and retreats.

Barbara Bartosh lives in Norman, OK with her cats. Her kids have wandered off to build lives. She works as a tax advisor/preparer for a firm in OKC. She enjoys writing, the community of believers she's been blessed with, studying, walking, road trips, and cuddles with her cats. It is a good life.

Contagious Overcomers
THIS IS HOW I FIGHT MY BATTLES

You Can Help

Contagious Overcomers is a 501 (c)(3), relying solely on donations to get our soul-saving content out to the masses. We are humbled, excited, and grateful for any funding you can provide. Donation summaries are mailed out each December. Thank you for your generosity and supporting the spreading of Kingdom principles in a broken world.

Make a Donation Today!

Paypal

Paypal accepts paypal or debit/credit cards. Reoccurring or one-time www.paypal.com/donate/?hosted_button_id=9SB9BE4NV3JQA

Venmo

@contagiousovercomers

Fidelity Charitable

Donate through your retirement www.fidelitycharitable.org/

Mail

Contagious Overcomers Ministry, PO Box 5434, Norman, OK 73070

www.ingramcontent.com/pod-product-compliance
Lightning Source LLC
LaVergne TN
LVHW080627160826
845677LV00007B/1471

* 9 7 9 8 9 8 5 8 5 2 8 2 0 *